Barbie® Doll Treasures

1959-1997

by Rebecca Ann Rupp

Published by

Hobby House Press, Inc.
Grantsville, Maryland 21536

FEATURES:
Fashion Booklets, Fashions, Dolls, Structures, & more...

DEDICATION

To my wonderful parents, thank you both for loving and encouraging me to have wings that propel me to the continuation and realization of my dreams. Also, to the sweet memory of my Grandmother — Annie Hendrick Cornwell, who wrote verse, poetry and song lyrics and from whom I inherited my talent.

ACKNOWLEDGEMENTS

Thank you to my mother, Jo Ann Cornwell Rupp for photographic assistance and my father, Richard Rupp for assistance.

A very special thank you to A. Glenn Mandeville.

I would like to take this opportunity to thank the following for their continuing help in my quest for two fully developed books: Wanda Brown, June Burton, Alice Chaney, Mary Colglazier, Jodi Drisbrow, Louise Henderson, Rosemary Kanizer, Betty Kaiser, Joy Koniak, Phyllis Key Lawson, Verna Monheimer, Louise Russell, Kitty Stuart, Pat Swanagin, Susan Watson, and Patty Wickering.

Throughout the years the following friends and family have sent me newspaper articles from across the United States. Thanks to each of you: Patsy Austin, Betty Bennett, Beatrice Boston, Sarah McCubbins, Marcia Larkin, Carrie Crisler Paar, Dot Tucker, and Dottie Sue Weed.

Front Cover: Top Right: The arabian stallion ***Prancer***™ (1984) with ***Loving You BARBIE***® doll. For more information see page 34. ***Middle Left: The World of Barbie Fashionsand Playthings*** by Mattel. For more information see page 50. ***Bottom Right: BARBIE® and Ken® Hot Rod*** (1963-1964). For more information see page 28.
Title Page: The *Enchanted Seasons Collection*®: ***Snow Princess***™ ***BARBIE***® doll, ***Spring Bouquet***® ***BARBIE***® doll, ***Autumn Glory***® ***BARBIE***® doll, ***Summer Splendor***™ ***BARBIE***® doll. For more information see page 4.
Back Cover: The Modern Olympic games celebrated the centennial anniversary in 1996. For more information see page 79. ***BARBIE® Dream Boat***™. For more information see page 29.

ABOUT THE AUTHOR

Rebecca Ann Rupp is a devoted BARBIE® doll fan! An avid BARBIE® club member, seminar and exhibit presenter, Rebecca loves to share her 27 years of BARBIE® doll collecting knowledge with others. She has participated in numerous television and radio interviews as well as national and regional convention presentations, including the well received slide presentation "Around the World with the International BARBIE® dolls" at the 1991 National BARBIE® Doll Convention.

In 1988, Rebecca's club, the Derby City Doll Club of Kentucky hosted a U.F.D.C. Region 8 conference, "Vive Les Bébés" where Rebecca's first exhibit "Welcome to BARBIE®town U.S.A." (the appellation she gave her collection at age nine) was featured.

Rebecca has served as chairperson of the "Fashionable BARBIE® Doll Luncheon"; editorial assistant and staff writer for "Vive Les Bébés" souvenir book as well as a contributing writer for various publications. She has also served as a judge at the National BARBIE® Doll Convention. A respected dealer and appraiser of modern collectible dolls, Rebecca's first book, ***Treasury of Barbie Doll Accessories*** was published in 1996.

Additional copies of this book may be purchased at $24.95 (plus postage and handling) from

Hobby House Press, Inc.
1 Corporate Drive
Grantsville, Maryland 21536
1-800-554-1447
or from your favorite bookstore or dealer.

Printed in the United States of America

ISBN: 0-87588-505-5

TABLE OF CONTENTS

See Chapter 1 for more information.

See Chapter 9 for more information.

Introduction

Thanks to all of you who purchased my first book, *Treasury of BARBIE® Doll Accessories 1961-1995.* Many of you have written to me or told me in person that you have enjoyed my work.

It was a pleasure meeting you and noting happily, the worn and used copies of my book carried by knowledgeable collectors.

1996 was a year filled with memorable highlights including: BARBIE® Doll and the Bandstand", the National BARBIE® Doll Convention in Philadelphia, PA and an exhibit of a small portion of my collection at Oxmoor Center in Louisville, KY.

The endeavor of this ensuing volume is to expand the horizons of the collector to the multi-dimensional world of BARBIE® doll, accessories, and fashions collecting.

1. Any season can be BARBIE® doll collecting season, for dolls, fashions, and accessories from 1959 to 1997 and beyond. Illustrated are the *Enchanted Seasons Collection®*: ***Snow Princess™ BARBIE®*** doll (1994), ***Spring Bouquet® BARBIE®*** doll (1995), ***Autumn Glory® BARBIE®*** doll (1996), ***Summer Splendor™ BARBIE®*** doll (1997). Dolls designed by Mattel, Inc. designer, Janet Goldblatt.

2. My first book ***Treasury of BARBIE® Doll Accessories 1961 to 1995*** debuted in February 1996. Throughout the year I participated in many book signings. Illustrated is an exhibit of "Welcome to BARBIE®town U.S.A." small portion of my collection at Oxmoor Center in Louisville, Kentucky. All attendees were thrilled to see some of the accessories featured in Volume I and to obtain an autographed copy of the book. *Photograph by Jo Ann Cornwell Rupp.*

Chapter 1

Memorable Moments

BARBIE® doll is the world's most renowned fashion doll with resilient longevity. Her most memorable moments include:

Inspired by her daughter's adult paper dolls and fashions, Ruth Handler created a three dimensional doll named BARBIE® after her daughter Barbara. BARBIE® doll debuted at the 1959 New York Toy Fair, receiving what some perceive as an unenthusiastic response. All this would change. In 1962 the BARBIE® Fan Club" began and by 1964 the club's membership boasted a half-million worldwide members.

The first reproduction doll, "Original BARBIE® doll", was offered in the 1972 Montgomery Ward & Company Christmas Catalogue for $2.77. This doll was an exclusive Montgomery Ward reproduction. A #5 doll was reproduced for Montgomery Ward's centennial anniversary.

"The International BARBIE® Collectors Club" was founded by Ruth Cronk. A newsletter entitled "The International Barbie Collectors Club Gazette" was produced from 1980 to 1988. Since 1980, this club has held annual National Barbie Conventions at various U.S. locations.

A new collector's series, "Porcelain Collection", began in 1987. Each of the six dolls were porcelain bisque and limited in number.

To commemorate Mattel's golden anniversary a porcelain bisque "50th -1945 to 1995 - Mattel Golden Anniversary BARBIE® doll" was issued.

3. Ruth Handler and Elliot Handler are shown in a 1962 photograph depicting the first four years of BARBIE® and Ken® dolls. Limited to an edition of 300, the photograph was singed by Ruth Handler and came with a certificate of authenticity. This item sold for $100.00 at the 1994 Limited Edition Sale, a part of the BARBIE® 35th Anniversary Festival. Rare.

4. "... and now — let's play with our BARBIE® dolls!" from a photo essay published in *The World of Barbie — The Barbie Magazine Annual* (1964). Collectors have a wide range to chose from: Skipper doll fashion, ***"Me 'N My Doll"*** (1965 to 1966) Rare. Tutti doll fashion, ***"Let's Play Barbie"*** doll (1967) Very, very rare. Each fashion came with miniature blonde Swirl BARBIE® dolls. *Miniatures by Rebecca Brasdahl.*

5. *The World of Barbie — The Barbie Magazine Annual,* published by Mattel, Inc., 1964. Allan Grant, a Life Magazine photographer, was the editor-in-chief and photographer for this annual. Pictured on the front cover is *#993 Sophisticated Lady* (1963-1964). Rare.

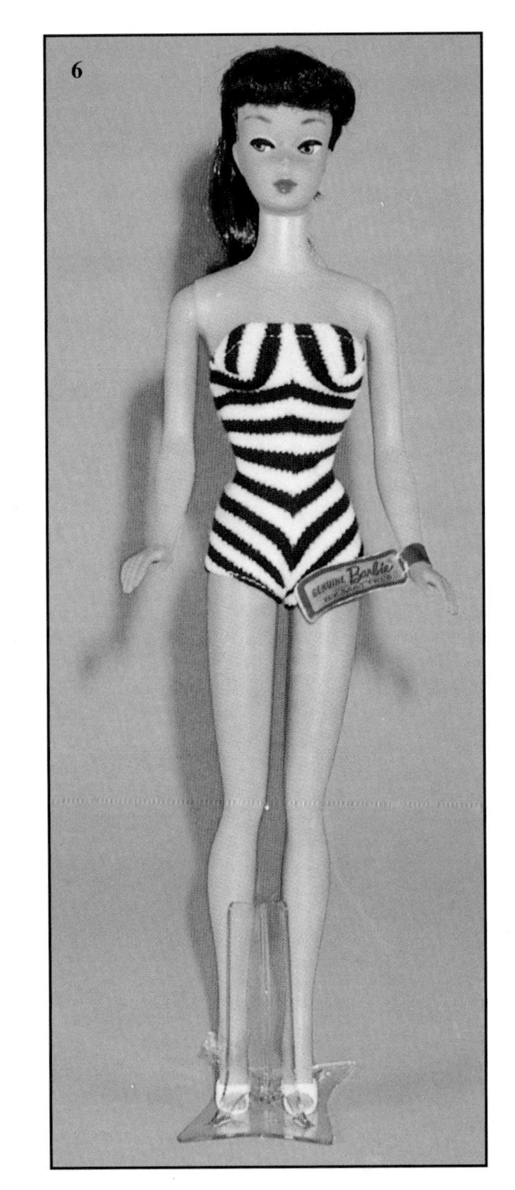

6. The ***Original BARBIE®*** doll was the first reproduction doll. An exclusive for Montgomery Wards. 1972. Very, very rare.

7. Various issues of ***The International BARBIE® Doll Collectors Club Gazette***. The club gazette was produced from 1980 through 1988. Also shown are the author's club membership cards.

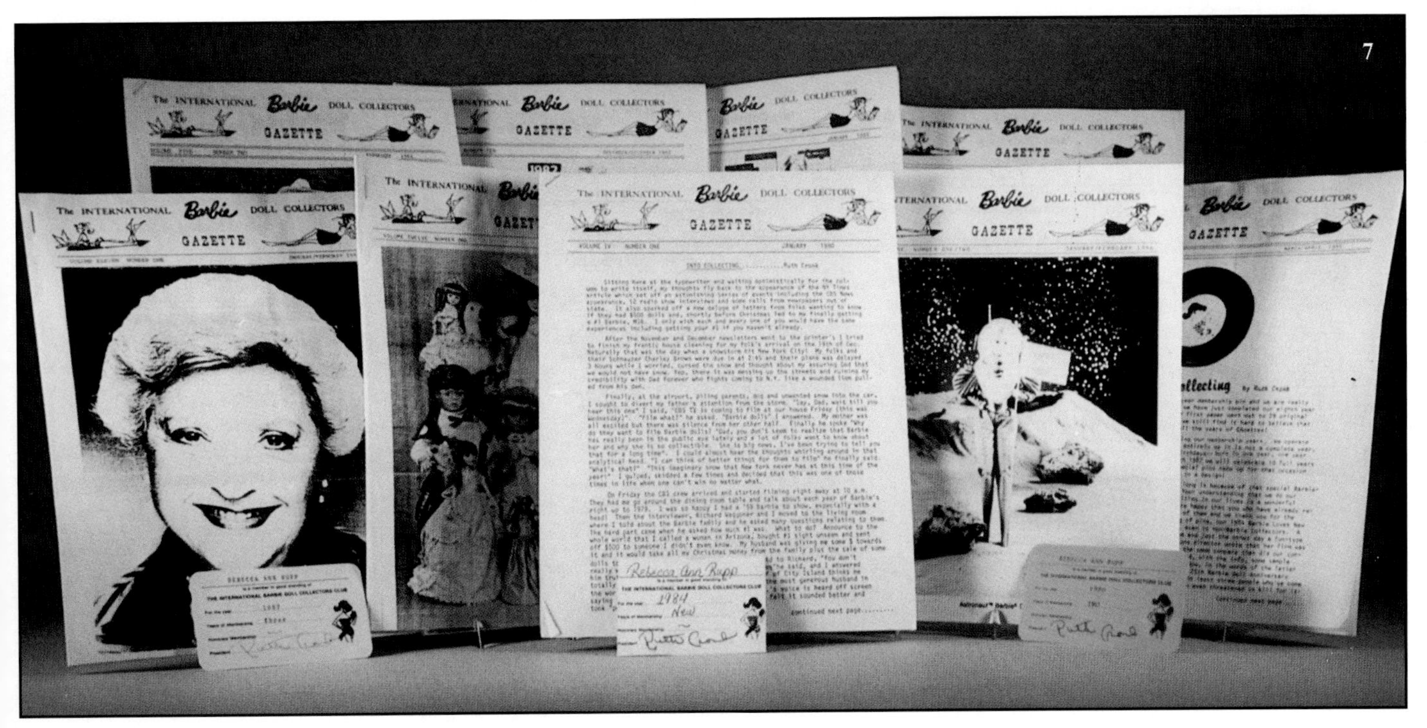

8

THE INTERNATIONAL BARBIE DOLL COLLECTOR'S CLUB

BARBIE LOVES NEW YORK

CONVENTION · 1984

8. The International Barbie Doll Collector's Club ***BARBIE® Loves New York*** 1984 convention souvenir book.

9. Sears 100th anniversary commemorative exclusive was ***Celebration™ BARBIE®*** doll (1985). Hard to find. Sears Roebuck and Co. featured very unique accessories, the majority of which are today rare and hard to find. For more information see Chapter 3 Rarest Architecture as well as *Treasury of BARBIE® Doll Accessories* page 31-35.

10. In April 1988, my club, Derby City Doll Club of Kentucky, presented their first U.F.D.C. Region 8 conference, "Vive Les Bébés", complete with a "Fashionable BARBIE® Doll Luncheon", which the author was chairperson. Pictured is the ***Fun-to-Dress BARBIE®*** doll (the luncheon centerpiece) in an adapted French fashion designed by Betty Ensor. Six lucky attendees took this doll home.

11. ***Blue Rhapsody***™ (1986) was the first porcelain bisque BARBIE® doll created by Mattel, Inc. A certificate and booklet were included. Limited to an edition of 6,000. Rare.

12. ***Enchanted Evening***™ (1987) was the second doll in the porcelain series. Limited to an edition of 10,000. This doll and fashion was the first nostalgic reproduction. Rare.

13. ***Benefit Performance***™ (1988) was the third doll in the porcelain series. Limited to an edition of 10,000. This doll was an adaptation of the 1967 Twist 'N Turn BARBIE® doll with chocolate bon-bon hair. The fashion is similar to the original 1966-1967 *#1667 Benefit Performance*. This doll was the only doll in the series to have eyelashes. Rare.

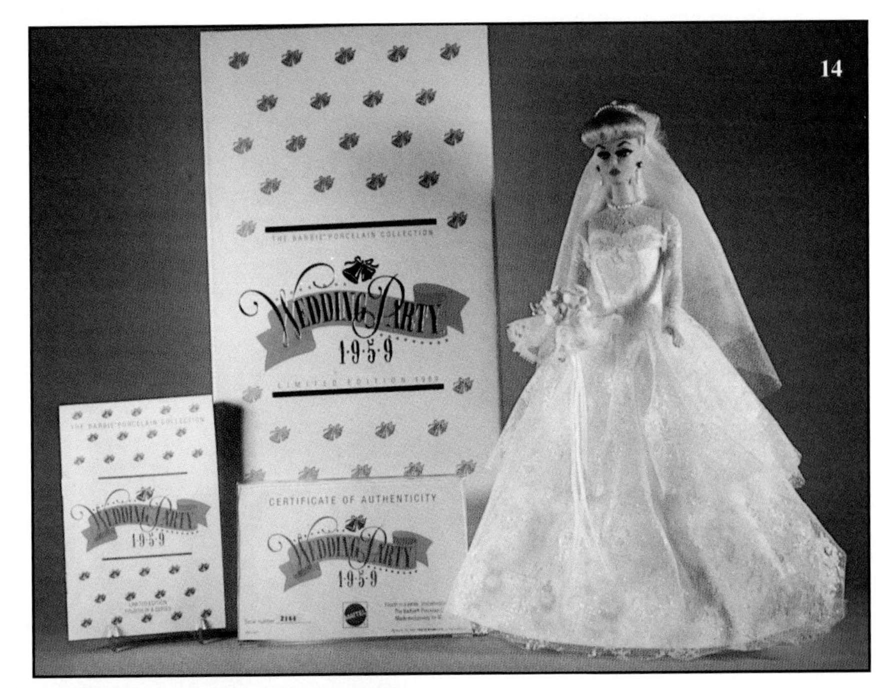

14. ***Wedding Party***™ (1989) and the 1959 BARBIE® doll was the fourth doll in the porcelain series. Limited to an edition of 10,000 worldwide. Adapted from the 1959 Wedding Party BARBIE® doll fashion and the doll aporcelain adaption of the #1 1959 BARBIE® doll. Rare.

15. ***Solo in the Spotlight***™ (1990) was the fifth doll in the porcelain series. Adapted from the 1961 Solo in the Spotlight BARBIE® doll fashion ensemble.

16. ***Sophisticated Lady***™ (1990) was the sixth doll in the porcelain series. Adapted from the 1965 Sophisticated Lady BARBIE® doll fashion.

17. ***Dance Magic™ BARBIE®*** doll has a special sticker-decal located on the window in the upper right corner to indicate that this was a souvenir doll from the 1990 BARBIE® Grants a Wish event which was presented by BARBIE® Doll Collector Club Great Lakes Chapter. As a centerpiece, this doll was surrounded by a pink cloud of cotton as shown.

18. The 1991 National BARBIE® Doll Convention's theme was "BARBIE® Loves A Fairy Tale" held in Omaha, Nebraska (event limited to 500 registrants). BARBIE® and Ken® doll's fairy tale costumes were designed by Steve Skutka. This was the first souvenir Ken doll at a National BARBIE® Doll Convention. 1991 was Ken® doll's 30th anniversary. Also shown is the souvenir book, table favors, and the author's name badge.

19. The 1994 National BARBIE® Doll Convention theme was "The Magic of BARBIE® in Birmingham" held in Alabama (event limited to 650 registrants). Shown are the souvenir doll, fashion, book, table favors, and the author's name badge.

20. Artist Catena Lemonakis created this print ***"The Magic of BARBIE® in Birmingham"*** especially for the 1994 convention. Convention attendees could purchase the 11-1/2" x 14-5/8" print and have the artist sign it. Limited to an edition of 600 prints. Shown with certificate of authenticity. This print was also used as the souvenir book cover.

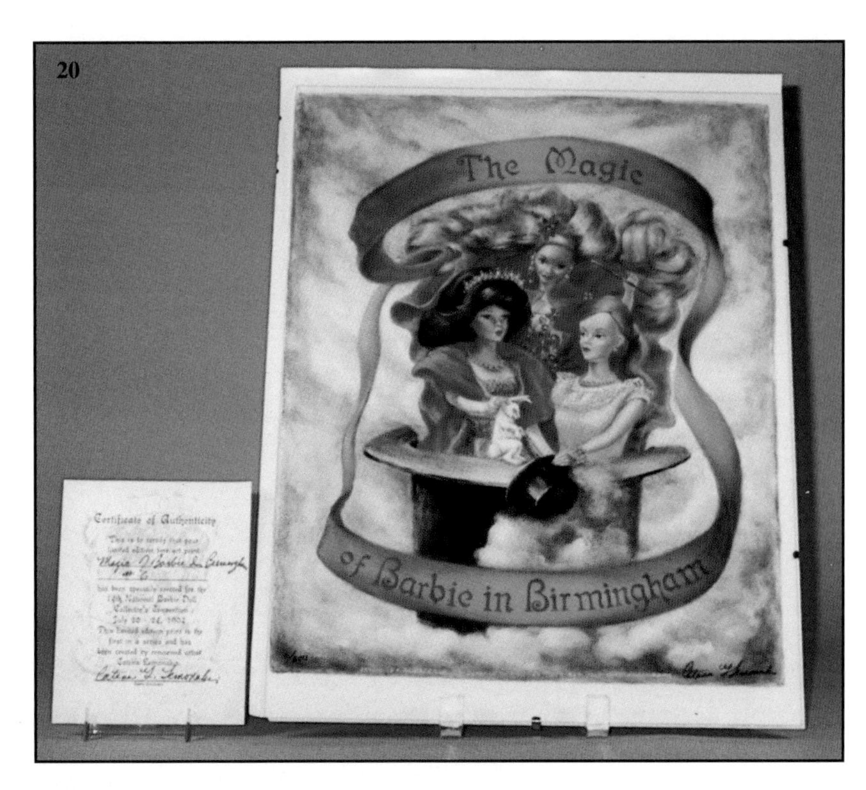

21. 50th 1945 to 1995 ***Golden Anniversary BARBIE®*** doll (1995)was created exclusively for Mattel's 50th anniversary. This bisque porcelain doll is dressed in Mattel's colors — red and gold. The red velvet evening gown is adorned with fifty red roses, one representing each year. The doll wears a 23kt gold electroplated bracelet with "Mattel" imprinted on one side and "50th" on the other. On the right is ***Mattel, Inc. 1994, Annual Report - Celebrating 50 Years***.

22. "BARBIE® and the Bandstand" National Convention memorabilia, 1996. Some items received at time of registration: ***BARBIE® Beat Convention Magazine***; ***BARBIE® Tune Tote***; ***BARBIE® Sings Autograph and Beehive!***; ***Autograph Book***; ***Tote bag***, etc. Other pictured items were received as table favors or at convention events. Also shown is the convention package and the author's name badge.

23. ***Bandstand Beauty BARBIE®*** doll was the souvenir doll for the 1996 National BARBIE® Doll Convention. It was the first time that a souvenir doll had a name rather than the convention title. The 1960's style singer was designed by Dick Tahsin and was limited to an edition of 800. A certificate of authenticity and a copy of the original sketch accompanied the doll; each of which, as well as the box was personally signed by the designer.

24

24. The ***BARBIE® Carrying Case*** was sold separately at the 1996 convention.

25. This compact disc, ***BARBIE® Sings 60's Style*** was produced exclusively for "BARBIE® And The Bandstand"; c. 1996 Delaware Valley BARBIE® Club Records. It was sold separately at the convention.

26

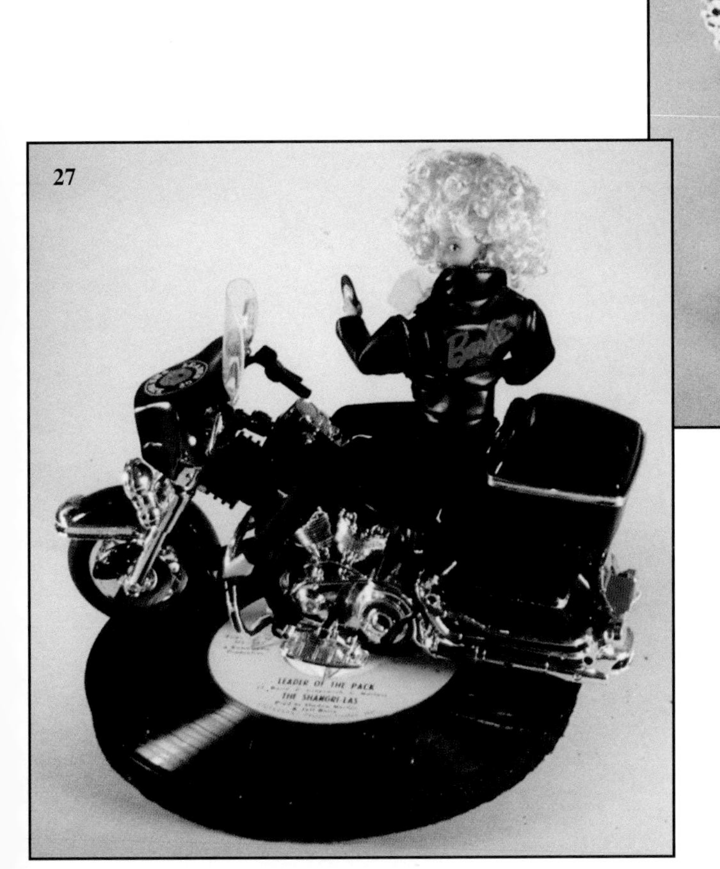

26 & 27. "BARBIE® And The Bandstand" had groovy musical themes at all the events. ***Leader of the Pack Luncheon Centerpiece*** was limited to an edition of 80. COOL is the word! The motorcycle actually makes motorcycle sounds, has working headlights, and taillights. A rear view shows BARBIE® doll's leatherette jacket with the signature logo on the back.

28. ***Dancin' Party*** was the centerpiece given to the 80 lucky table hostesses at "BARBIE® and The Bandstand". Hard to find. Note: The tune tote has the same graphic on both sides unlike the convention souvenir tune tote. The miniature tune tote which BARBIE® doll is carrying has the same graphic which appears only on one side. The convention theme colors, as well as the dresses on the centerpieces, were in pink (as illustrated), yellow, and teal.

Chapter 2

BIRTHDAYS AND ANNIVERSARIES

BARBIE® doll was debuted at the New York Toy Fair on March 9, 1959 , yet it was 1975 before Mattel publicized her sweet sixteen. 1984, BARBIE® doll's 25th birthday was the last celebrated birthday. Since then, "birthdays" have been referred to as "anniversaries". Mattel's reasoning for changing the terminology was to not "age" BARBIE® doll and maintain youthfulness in the eyes of children. This strategy has been successful.

For more information on birthdays and anniversaries, see *Treasury of BARBIE® Doll Accessories*, Chapter 19, "Commemorative Merchandise".

29. Through the years BARBIE® doll has celebrated birthdays and anniversaries. BARBIE® doll has had the longest consecutive years of production by a single manufacturer in doll history.

30. BARBIE® doll celebrated her 16th birthday in 1974. Mattel issued ***Barbie's Sweet 16*** to commemorate the occasion.

31. BARBIE® doll celebrated her 21st birthday in 1980. The unofficial commemorative doll was, ***Kissing BARBIE®*** (1978). When pressing a panel in the doll's back, she tilts her head, puckers up and kisses with a kissing sound as the panel is released. The chiffon dress has a flower print with kissing lip marks. Hard to find.

32. A news story, "BARBIE® Turns 21" was reported in *Life Magazine* in regards to BARBIE® doll's 21st birthday.

33. BARBIE® doll celebrated her 25th anniversary in 1984. Although there was no official doll issued, who better to celebrate the occasion than ***Crystal BARBIE®*** and ***Crystal Ken®*** dolls?

34. ***BARBIE® Silver 'Vette*** (1984). The trendy shade of silver was available in various makes and models of mid-to-late '80s vehicles. This particular Corvette with a hatchback and roll bar was specifically for BARBIE® doll's silver anniversary. Hard to find.

35. ***Crystal BARBIE®*** and ***Crystal Ken®*** dolls (both 1984) unofficially celebrated BARBIE® doll's 25th anniversary out on the town in the ***BARBIE® Silver 'Vette*** (1984).

36

36. ***Collector Series III — Silver Sensation*** (1984) was the 25th anniversary fashion. Hard to find.

37. The advertisement for ***Blue Rhapsody***™ BARBIE® doll (1986) proclaimed the celebration of 27 years of BARBIE® doll glamour and excitement. For more information about this doll see illustration 11, page 10. Rare.

38. ***SuperStar BARBIE***® doll unofficially commemorated the 30th anniversary in 1989. ***SuperStar Ken***® doll was by her side to celebrate.

39. ***Wedding Party***™ ***1959 BARBIE***® doll (1989) commemorated the 30th anniversary. Mattel recreated a doll in porcelain to reflect the original 1959 BARBIE® doll, including the holes in the bottom of her feet. Her costume is the reproduced *#972 Wedding Day Set* ensemble.

40. BARBIE® doll celebrated her 30th anniversary in 1989. This advertisement illustrates a F.A.O. Schwarz limited edition exclusive for $45.00. Interestingly, the specific BARBIE® doll name is not given in the advertisement and the box does not mention that ***Golden Greetings™ BARBIE®*** doll is an F.A.O. Schwarz exclusive.

41. The brunette ***35th Anniversary BARBIE®*** doll was a 1994 reproduction to commemorate the first BARBIE® doll. In 1995, the Hallmark Keepsake Ornament Collector's Club exclusive was, ***BARBIE® Brunette Debut — 1959***.

42. ***35th Anniversary BARBIE® — Blonde*** and ***35th Anniversary BARBIE® — Blonde, Gift Set*** were reproductions issued in 1994 to commemorate the 35th anniversary of the first BARBIE® doll.

43. ***35th Anniversary Festival BARBIE®*** doll with hangtag and certificate of authenticity was limited to an edition of 3,500 for the 1994 35th Anniversary Festival. This doll was available at the Limited Edition Sale for $125. Rare.

44. The 1991 ***30th Anniversary — 1961 Ken®*** doll was recreated in porcelain bisque. The doll style replicates the original flocked crew cut hairstyle and the early *#787 Tuxedo* fashion. Hard to find.

45. ***30th Anniversary - 1964 Skipper*** doll (1994) was a commemorative porcelain bisque replica of BARBIE® doll's little sister. Her costume replicates the 1965 fashion *#1919 Happy Birthday*. Hard to find.

Chapter 3

The Rarest Architecture

There are several hard to find and/or rare architecture structures for scene presentations manufactured throughout the years. The rarest of rare architecture was produced before 1972. These items, which are at the top of the collector's accessory wish list, are illustrated here. For more information on structres see *Treasury of BARBIE® Doll Accessories 1961-1995*.

46. ***BARBIE® and Ken® Little Theater*** (1964). Rare. The performance pictured on the stage is entitled "King Arthur's Adventure" from the play scripts booklet. The stars of the show wear the Little Theater Costumes, Ken® doll as "King Arthur" (1964-1965); BARBIE® doll as "Guinevere" (1964-1965).

Left: 47 & 48. The paperboard ***BARBIE® and Skipper School*** (1965) was made exclusively for Sears. Very rare.

Above: 49. The exterior graphic of the ***BARBIE® and Skipper School*** (1965) show a school bus and school house. When folded-in, this structure could be carried. Very rare.

50. Inside the ***BARBIE® and Skipper School*** classroom (1965). Very rare.

51. The reverse side of the ***BARBIE® and Skipper School*** (1965) showed a school yard. Very rare.

52. ***Skipper Dream Room*** (1965-1966). Rare. Also shown is a Skipper doll with "Lifelike Bendable Legs" (1965) wearing *Rainy Day Checkers* (1966). Hard to find.

53. ***Skipper Dream Room*** interior. Skipper doll wears *Dreamtime* (1964-1966), while friend Skooter doll wears *Skipper Fashion Pak — Wooly P.J.'s* (1965-1967).

54 & 55. The ***Skipper Dream Room*** has more parts than any of the other paperboard architecture produced. Notice the table top has a graphic of a "BARBIE®'s Little Sister, Skipper Game" and the dollhouse was "BARBIE®'s New Dream House".

56. ***BARBIE® Goes to College — Campus*** (1964-1965) was a Sears exclusive. Rare.

57. The ***BARBIE® Goes to College — Campus*** folds-out to five settings, two of which were on one side and can be seen here — the dormitory room and the Campus Sweet Shop. 1964 to 1965. Very rare.

58. Cheering for the Mattel team in front of the football field graphic-exterior of ***BARBIE® Goes to College — Campus*** structure are BARBIE® doll wearing *Cheerleader* (1964-1965); and Ken® doll wearing *Campus Hero* (1961-1964).

59. Here is the BARBIE® and Midge dolls' dormitory room portion of ***BARBIE® Goes to College — Campus*** (1964-1965). Rare.

60. After the homecoming game, BARBIE® doll and friends can go to the Campus Sweet Shop portion of ***BARBIE® Goes to College — Campus*** (1964-1965). Rare.

61. This portion of the ***BARBIE® Goes to College - Campus*** shows the Campus Drive-In Theater. The movie playing on the screen was Cinderella starring BARBIE® and Ken® dolls. The BARBIE® doll vehicles shown, ***BARBIE®'s Sports Car*** and ***BARBIE® and Ken® Hot Rod*** did not come with this accessory. Rare.

62. The ***BARBIE® Café Today***™ (1971), has a carrying handle. Very rare. Also shown, a "Twist 'N Turn BARBIE® doll" (1969 issue) wearing *Ruffles 'N Swirls* (1970).

63. ***Live Action BARBIE®*** doll (1971-1973); ***Live Action Ken®*** doll (1971-1973); and ***Live Action P.J.*** doll (1971-1973) could have a groovy time in the ***BARBIE® Café Today***™ structure (1971). It was decorated in MODern colors. Very rare.

Chapter 4

LEISURE ACTIVITIES

The leisure time fun of BARBIE® doll has included recreational pursuits such as cruising in the "BARBIE® and Ken® Hot Rod", camping and sailing. Not only is BARBIE® doll current in fashion and trends, but she enjoys the popular leisure activities of the time.

64. ***BARBIE® and Ken® Hot Rod*** (1963-1964) was made by the Irwin Corporation under license from Mattel, Inc. Rare.

65. The hottest camper on wheels was the ***BARBIE® Country Camper***™ (1971-1976). Vacationing were *Dramatic New Living BARBIE®* doll (1970), *New Living Skipper* doll (1970), and *Talking Ken®* doll wearing the *Shore Lines* fashion (1970).

66 & 67. There were two versions of ***BARBIE®'s Pool Party***. The first version with the basic pool was copyrighted 1973. The second version had "added features" (a plastic patio mat) and was copyrighted 1974.

68. ***BARBIE® Sunsailer™*** (1975) was styled after a real Hobie Cat® (registered trademark of Coast Catamaran Corp.). This three foot high sailboat could float and featured an adjustable mainsail and tiller. It was made for one year. Rare.

69. ***BARBIE® Dream Boat™*** (1975-1976). This yacht was styled to a real Chris Craft®. It opens to four feet, one inch long. Hard to find.

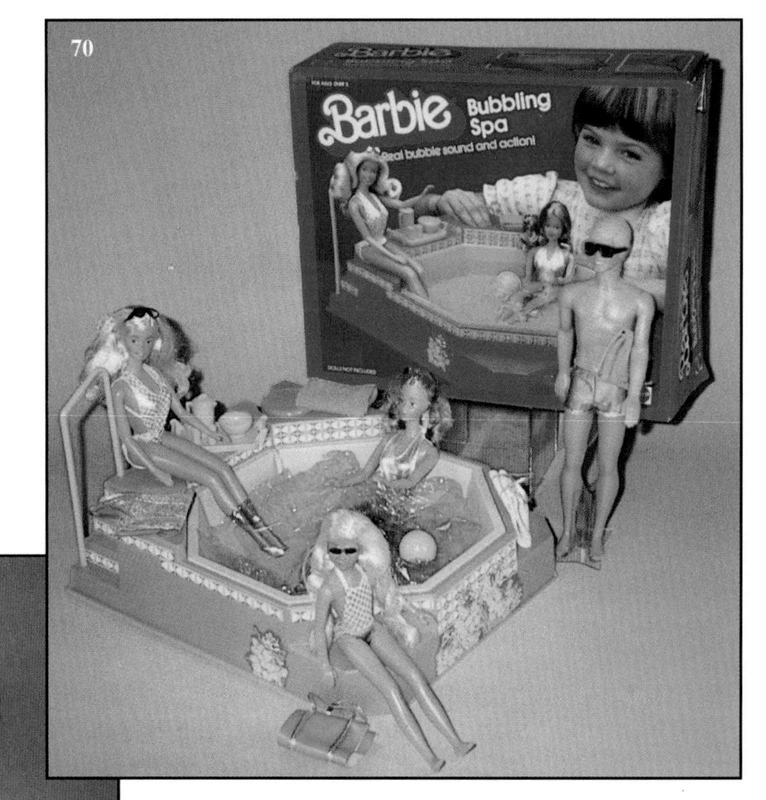

70. ***BARBIE® Bubbling Spa*** (1984). Hard to Find. When the hand pump was pumped the spa bubbled and made realistic sounds. Joining *Sun Gold—Malibu®* BARBIE® doll in the hot-tub was *Sun Gold—Malibu® P.J. doll*, hard to find; *Sun Gold—Malibu® Skipper* doll, hard to find; and *Sun Gold—Malibu® Ken®* doll.

71. ***BARBIE® Motor Bike*** (1984).

72. The Toys R Us exclusive ***BARBIE® & Ken® doll Tennis Stars™ Gift Set*** (1988) came with a tennis net — unlike the European versions, *Tennis BARBIE®* doll, *Tennis Ken®* doll, and *Tennis Skipper* doll (1987).

73 & 74. ***Ken® So Much To Do! Weight Liftin' Fun*** (1995) and ***Ken® So Much to Do! Surfin' Action*** (1995).

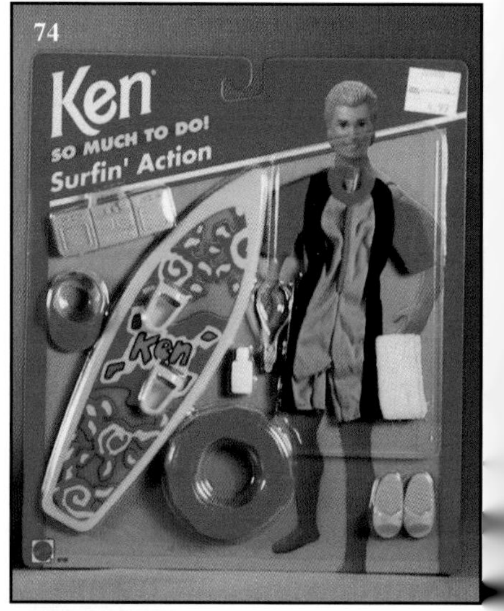

75. ***BARBIE® Mini Van*** (1996-still available in 1997). This is the first BARBIE® doll vehicle to have open/close doors.

Chapter 5

THE IMAGE OF EQUINE

BARBIE® doll has had a menagerie of pets throughout the years. The very first pet, a horse named Dancer™ was introduced in 1971 . Since that time there have been a number of accessories with the equine theme.

The following horses have been available in the United States:

1971	*Dancer*™
1981-1984	*Dallas*™ *Golden Palomino*
1982	*Midnight*™ *Stallion*
1983	*Honey*™ (Skipper doll's pony)
1984	*Dixie*™ *Palomino Colt* (off-spring mare of *Dallas*™ and *Midnight*™)
1988	*Prancer*™ *Arabian Stallion*
1988	*Blinking Beauty*™
1990	*Sun Runner*™
1991	*All-American*™
1991	*Snow Flake*™
1992	*Rosebud*
1993	*Western Star*™
1994-1996	*High Stepper*®
1996	*Nibbles*™

For more information about other pets, see *Treasury of BARBIE® Doll Accessories 1961 - 1995*, Chapter 11, "The Pet Menagerie".

76. ***Dancer***™ (1971). This chocolate colored horse has jointed legs. Its hoofs, when bent, can make hoof beat sounds. It can also rear back and race on the hand controlled rocker stand. Rare.

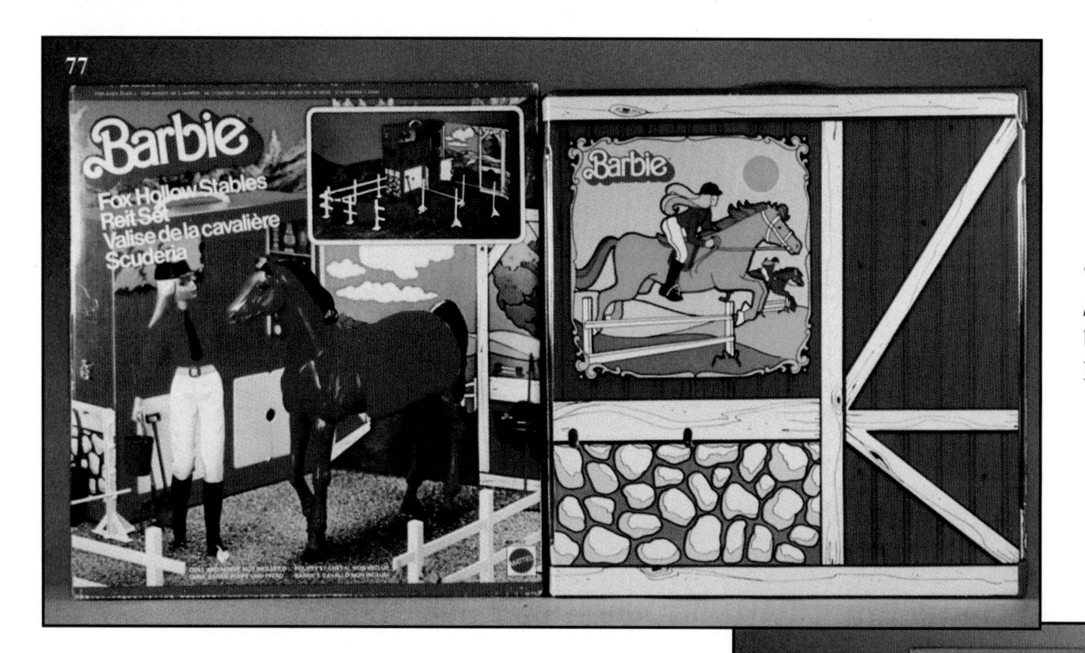

77. ***BARBIE® Fox Hollow Stables*** (1977) was available in both West Germany and France. Rare.

78. ***Dallas***™, a golden palomino horse (1981-1984) poses with ***Western BARBIE®*** doll (1981-1982) who winks her left eye.

79. ***Midnight***™, a black stallion (1982-1984) poses with ***Western Ken®*** doll (1981-1982).

80 & 81. *BARBIE® & Ken® Western Fashions* — ***Western Elegance!*** and ***Western Fringe!*** (both 1981).

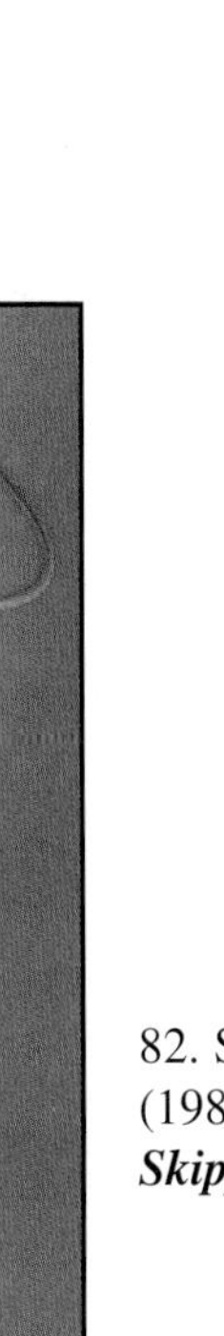

83. *BARBIE® Designer Collection*, ***Horseback Riding*** (1983).

82. Show pony ***Honey***™ (1983) poses with ***Western Skipper*** doll (1982). Rare.

84. ***Dream Horse***™ ***Dixie***™, BARBIE® doll's baby palomino (1984). The certificate of registration announces the Sire's name: Midnight; and the Dam's name: Dallas. Rare.

85. The arabian stallion ***Prancer***™ (1984) poses with ***Loving You BARBIE***® doll. Hard to find.

86. ***Western Fun***™ ***BARBIE***® doll (1990) is shown on ***Western Fun***™ ***Sun Runner***™ (1990). Hard to Find. This southwestern scene also shows BARBIE® doll's friend, ***Western Fun***™ ***Nia*** doll (1990), rare; ***Western Fun***™ ***Ken***® doll (1990); and Western Fun™ BARBIE® doll's pet collie, ***Turquoise***™ (1990). Rare.

87. ***BARBIE***® ***Dream Carriage/Sleigh*** (1991) from Italy. This unique accessory transforms from a carriage (as shown) to a sleigh. Hard to find.

88. The ***BARBIE® Dream Carriage/Sleigh*** (1991) from Italy as a sleigh. Hard to find.

89. ***Dear BARBIE® Riding Champion*** (1995). A Golden Book - Western Publishing Company, Inc, printed under license. This storybook by L.L. Hitchcock has BARBIE® doll and Skipper doll participating in a state fair horse show.

90. ***Western Stampin'™ BARBIE®*** doll with ***Western Star Horse*** (1995). The box advertises: "Stamp trails of fun with BARBIE® doll's boots and horse hooves!"

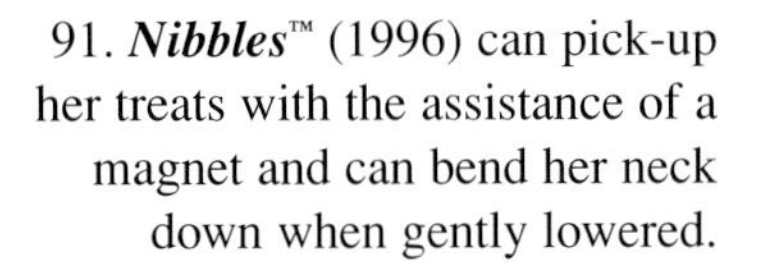

91. ***Nibbles***™ (1996) can pick-up her treats with the assistance of a magnet and can bend her neck down when gently lowered.

92. ***Nibbles***™ (1996-1997) and the ***BARBIE® Feeding Fun Stable***™ (1996-1997). See "How to Guide for Collectors on Scene Composition & Tips" page 117 for scene setting information.

93. ***BARBIE® Songbird Horse & Carriage/Carruaje Dulces Canciones/ Cheval et Cale'che Joli Rossignal*** (1996) received global distribution. The prancing horse really pulls the carriage and the bird's wings flutter. The box's photo-art captures these movements. This item requires two C Alkaline batteries to function.

94. ***BARBIE® Sweet Magnolia™ Horse & Carriage Set*** (c. 1996) was the first accessory exclusive for Wal-Mart. The store received limited quantities for the holiday season. The item was shortly thereafter discontinued. Behind the reigns is Wal-Mart exclusive, ***Sweet Magnolia™ BARBIE®*** doll (1996).

BARBIE® Fashions as Seen on *LIFE* Magazine — August 23, 1963

BARBIE® doll modeled her wardrobe for *Life* magazine five years after her debut. A three page story in the August 23, 1963 issue "BARBIE® Doll's Huge Success — The Most Popular Doll In Town" showcased "BARBIE®'s $136 wardrobe from nurse to nightclubber". The feature was written by Allan Grant, who in 1964 became the editor-in-chief and photographer for *The World of BARBIE® — The BARBIE® Doll Magazine Annual*.

The article slated Mattel, Inc. as the largest toy company and the biggest clothing manufacturer in number of outfits produced. The first page of the article (page 73) featured an actual size photograph of a blonde bubblecut BARBIE® doll wearing *#954 Career Girl* fashion. The next two pages (pages 74-75) was devoted to "BARBIE®'s $136.00 Wardrobe". A brief description was provided but the main focus was the photograph of 64 dolls modeling the then available fashions along with some discontinued outfits. The wardrobe included the #900 Series fashions (which in mint and complete condition are currently estimated at $3,960!) as well as the Mix 'N Match Fashion Paks. These fashions were also illustrated on a variety of items — cases, trunks, lunch boxes, insulated bottles, paper doll outfits, comic books, story books, etc., (for more information on these collectibles see *Treasury of BARBIE® Doll Accessories 1961 to 1995*). In recent years the #900 Series fashions have been illustrated and produced on such items as "Nostalgic" BARBIE® doll merchandise.

MODERN LIVING

The Most Popular Doll in Town

95. ***#954 Career Girl*** was the introductory fashion of the *Life* magazine article.

96. The article featured "BARBIE®'s $136 wardrobe from nurse to nightclubber" which included the 1963 fashion ensembles ***#991 Registered Nurse*** to ***#982 Solo In the Spotlight***.

97. ***#965 Nighty Negligee*** (1959-1964) was one of the pictured fashions. Hard to find with felt toy dog.

98. ***#921 Floral Petticoat*** (1959-1963) was also featured.

99. ***#973 Sweet Dreams*** (Yellow) (1959-1963). Hard to find with all pieces.

100. ***#943 Fancy Free*** (1963-1964).

101. ***#975 Winter Holiday*** (1959-1963). Hard to find.

102. ***#931 Garden Party*** (1962-1963).

103. ***#988 Singing In The Shower*** (1961-1963). This fashion is hard to find complete with all pieces — pink soap bar with initial "B" and talc powder box with powder puff.

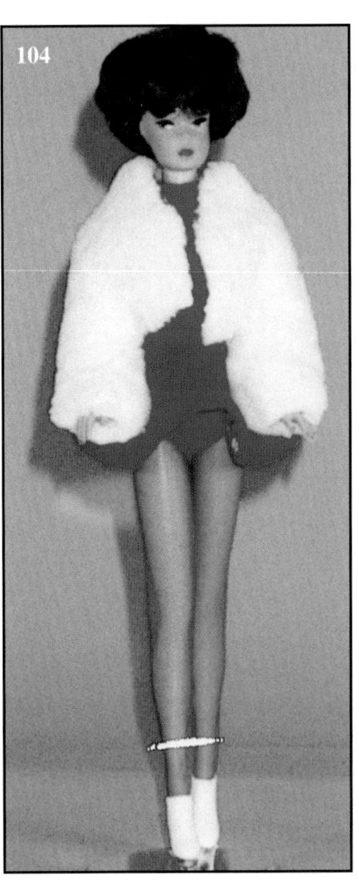

104. ***#942 Ice Breaker*** (1962-1964).

105. ***Left: #961 Evening Splendor*** (1959-1964). ***Right: #992 Golden Elegance*** (1963). Rare. The complete ensemble is hard to find.

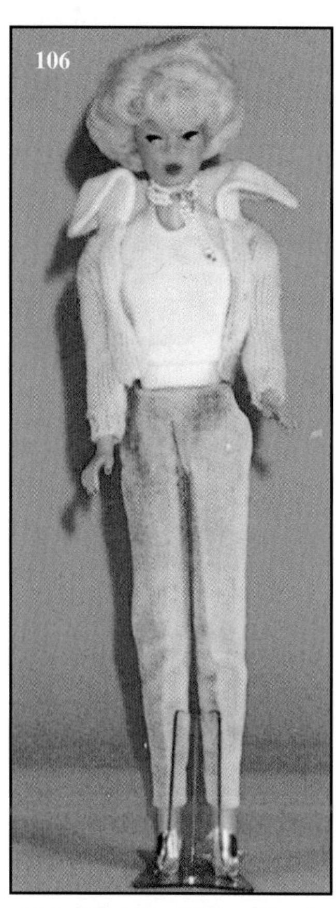

106. ***#940 Mood For Music*** (1962-1963). Hard to find.

107. ***#946 Dinner At Eight*** (1963-1964). Hard to find.

108. ***#958 Party Date*** (1963). Hard to find complete.

109. ***#951 Senior Prom*** (1963-1964). Hard to find complete with the rare green open toe shoes with pearls.

110. ***#949 Rain Coat*** (1963).

111. ***#933 Movie Date*** (1962-1963).

112. ***#915 Peachy Fleecy Coat*** (1959-1961). Hard to find complete with the feather on the hat.

113. ***#955 Swingin' Easy*** (1963). Hard to find with the drop-pearl on a chain necklace.

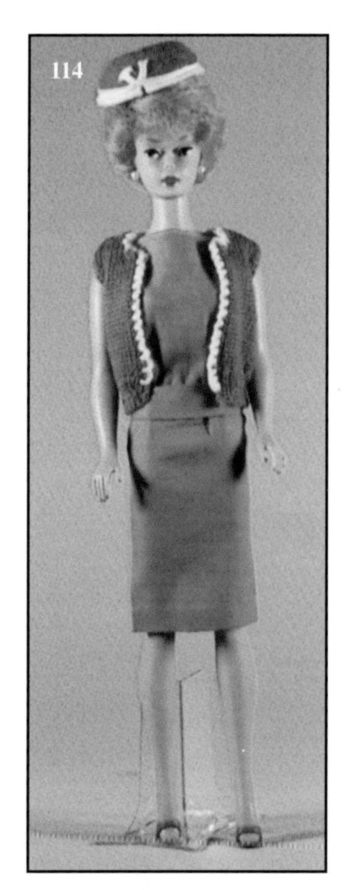

114. ***#937 Sorority Meeting*** (1962-1963).

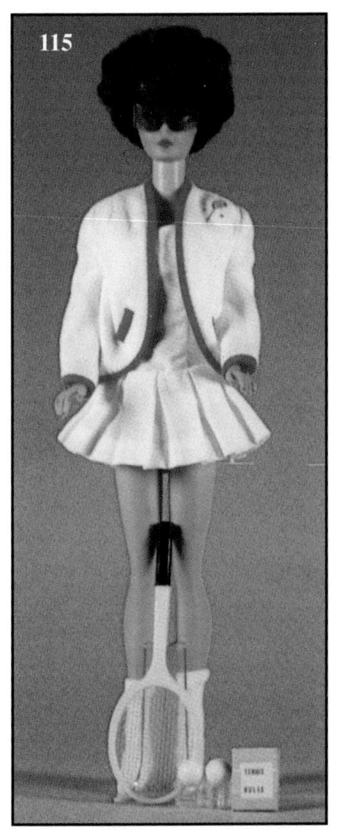

115. ***#941 Tennis Anyone?*** (1962-1964). Hard to find with all pieces — tennis racket, two tennis balls and Tennis Rules book.

116. ***#987 Orange Blossom*** (1961-1964). Hard to find with hat and bouquet.

117. ***#944 Masquerade*** (1963-1964). Hard to find.

118. ***#959 Theatre Date*** (1963). Hard to find with hat.

119. ***#984 American Airlines Stewardess*** (1961-1964). Hard to find complete ensemble — flight wings pin on jacket, hat with logo pin, and flight bag.

120. ***#945 Graduation*** (1963-1964). Hard to find with the diploma.

121. ***#983 Enchanted Evening*** (1960-1963). Hard to find with pearl jewelry.

122. ***#967 Picnic Set*** (1959-1961). Hard to find with rare fishing pole with the fish attached, hat and picnic basket.

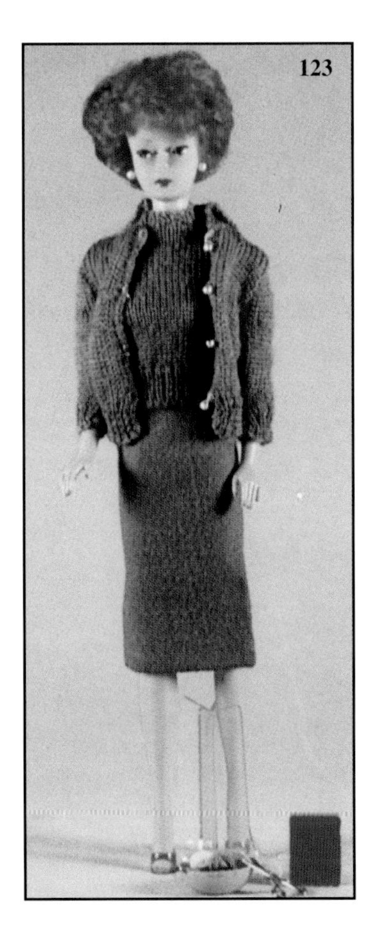

123. ***#957 Knitting Pretty*** (Navy) (1963).

124. ***#989 Ballerina*** (1961-1965). Hard to find the complete ensemble.

125. ***#948 Ski Queen*** (1963-1964). Hard to find with rare ski poles, skis and goggles.

126. ***#953 BARBIE® Baby-sits*** (1963-1964). Rare and hard to find complete with all pieces.

127. ***#956 Busy Morning*** (1963).

128. ***#934 After Five*** (1962-1964).

129. ***#979 Friday Night Date*** (1960-1964).

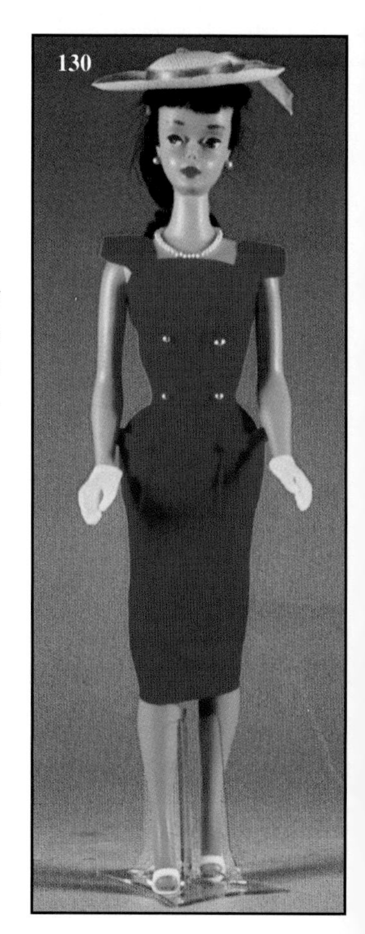

130. ***#986 Sheath Sensation*** (1961-1964).

131. ***#993 Sophisticated Lady*** (1963-1964).

132. ***#939 Red Flare*** (1962-1965). Hard to find with the purse rhinestone closure.

133. ***#947 Bride's Dream*** (1963-1965).

Chapter 7

FASHION BOOKLETS 1959 TO 1997

Fashion Booklets are promotional brochures featuring the dolls, fashions, and accessories of a certain time period. The illustrations usually feature a drawing or photograph of an item's prototype. Fashion Booklets originally came in the doll box or fashion package.

The following is a chronological list of fashion booklets, their copyright date (some were not dated) and noteworthy information:

1959

BARBIE® Teen-age Fashion Model, c.MCMLVIII featured the three rarest BARBIE® doll fashions, *Easter Parade*, *Gay Parisenne* and *Roman Holiday*.

BARBIE® Teen-age Fashion Model, c.MCMLVIII was the last fashion booklet to feature *Commuter Set*.

1960

BARBIE® Teen-age Fashion Model, c. MCMLVIII featured the same cover as the previously mentioned fashion booklets.

1961

134. "BARBIE® Teen-Age Fashion Model" c. MCMLV III. There were three fashion booklets in 1959 and 1960; each featured the same cover art.

BARBIE® Teen-age Fashion Model and BARBIE®'s Boyfriend, Ken® He's a Doll, c. 1961. There were two fashion booklets — one dated; the other not. Both had pink covers.

1962

BARBIE® Teen-age Fashion Model and BARBIE®'s Boyfriend Ken® He's a Doll, c. 1962. There were two fashion booklets — one dated; the other not. Both had light blue covers.

1963

BARBIE® Teen-age Fashion Model and BARBIE®'s Boyfriend Ken® He's a Doll! and BARBIE®'s Best Friend™ Midge, c. 1962. There were three fashion booklets. The covers were white, yellow and blue.

1964

BARBIE®, Ken®, Midge, Allan, and Skipper Exclusive Fashions by Mattel, c.1963. This was a series of four numbered books — Book 1, Book 2, Book 3 and Book 4.

Junior Edition Styles for Skipper BARBIE®'s Little Sister, c. 1963.

1965

BARBIE®, Ken®, Midge, Allan, Skipper, and Skooter Exclusive Fashions by Mattel, c.1964. This was a series of four numbered books — Book 1, Book 2, Book 3 and Book 4.

Junior Edition Styles for Skipper BARBIE®'s Little Sister - Skipper's Friends Skooter™ and Ricky™, c. 1964.

135. ***BARBIE® Teen-age Fashion Model and BARBIE®'s Boyfriend Ken® He's A Doll***, c. 1961 (pink covers).

136. ***BARBIE® Teen-age Fashion Model and BARBIE®'s Boyfriend Ken® He's a Doll***, c. 1962 (light blue covers).

137. These pamphlets — ***The BARBIE® Game Queen of the Prom***; ***Now BARBIE® Sings!***; and ***BARBIE® Dream House*** — were inserted in the Fashion Booklets of the early 1960s.

1966

The World of BARBIE® Fashions and Playthings by Mattel, c.1965. This was a series of four numbered books — Book 1, Book 2, Book 3 and Book 4.

Tutti™ — BARBIE®'s and Skipper's Tiny Sister, c. 1965.

Francie™ — BARBIE®'s MOD'ern Cousin, c. 1965.

1967

The World of BARBIE® Fashions by Mattel, c. 1966. There were four fashion booklets — one which was unnumbered and the other three numbered consecutively — Book 1, Book 2 and Book 3. Each cover featured illustrations of BARBIE®, Casey, Francie, Skipper, and Tutti dolls.

1968

The World of BARBIE® Fashions, c. 1967. This was a series of three numbered books — Book 1, Book 2, and Book 3.

1969

BARBIE®'s World: Bright, Swinging, Now., c.1968.

The World of BARBIE® Fashions, c.1968. This was a series of three numbered books — Book 1, Book 2 and Book 3.

1970

Living BARBIE® As Full of Life As You Are., c. 1969.

1971

Living BARBIE® and Skipper, c.1970. There were two cover variations — one says "'Join the New BARBIE® Fan Club Today!" and the other says "See letter from BARBIE® in back cover".

1972

The Lively World of BARBIE®, c. 1971.

1973

The Beautiful World of BARBIE®, c. 1972.

1974

The Beautiful World of BARBIE®, c. 1973. This fashion booklet featured the same photo-art illustration as the previous year.

138. These 1963 Fashion Booklets ***BARBIE® Teen-age Fashion Model™ and BARBIE®'s Boyfriend™ Ken® He's a doll!™ and BARBIE®'s Best Friend™ Midge*** feature the same cover illustration with different background colors (white, yellow, and blue).

1977

World of BARBIE® Fashions, c. 1976.

1978

BARBIE® World of Fashions, c.1978.

1979

BARBIE® World of Fashions, c. 1979. There were two editions —#007-2750 (A) and #0007-2750 (B).

1980

BARBIE® World of Fashion, c.1980.

1981

BARBIE® World of Fashion, c.1981. There were two editions —#007-3130 and #0007-3130 G3.

1982

BARBIE® World of Fashion, c. 1982. There were two editions —#0007-4100 and #0007-4100-G1.

My First BARBIE®, c.1982.

1983

BARBIE® World of Fashion, c. 1983.

1984

BARBIE® World of Fashion, c. 1984. There were two editions #0007-4680-G1 and #007-4680-G2.

1985

BARBIE® World of Fashion — We Girls Can Do Anything...Right, BARBIE®, c. 1984.

1986

BARBIE® World of Fashion — We Girls Can Do Anything...Right, BARBIE®, c. 1985.

1987

BARBIE® World of Fashion, c. 1987.

My First BARBIE®, c. 1986.

139 & 140. ***Exclusive Fashions by Mattel*** booklets were numbered — Book 1, Book 2, Book 3 and Book 4, 1963.

141. This pamphlet was for *New! Skipper — BARBIE®'s Little Sister*, c. 1963.

142. ***"Junior Edition" Styles for Skipper, Skooter & Ricky***, c. 1963.

143. ***Exclusive Fashions By Mattel*** Book 1 and Book 2, c. 1964.

145. ***The World of Barbie Fashions and Playthings*** by Mattel. c. 1965.

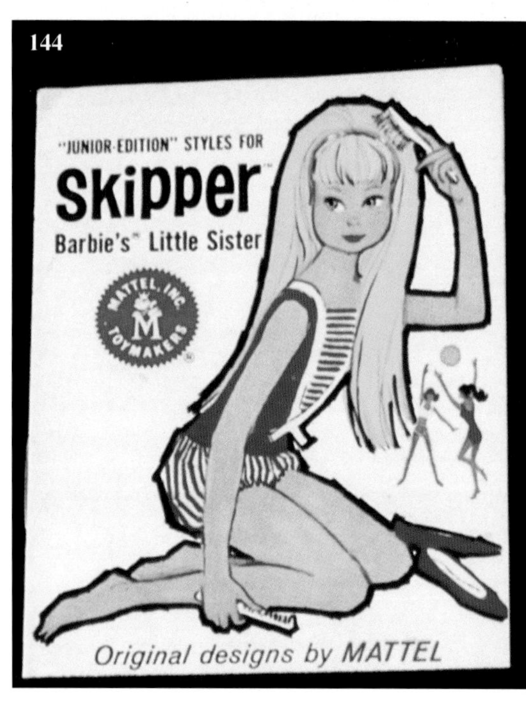

144. ***"Junior Edition" Styles for Skipper, BARBIE®'s Little Sister***, c. 1963.

146. ***Tutti™ — BARBIE® and Skipper's Tiny Sister***, c. 1965 and ***Francie™ BARBIE®'s MOD'ern Cousin***, c. 1965.

1988

BARBIE® World of Fashion, c. 1988.

Skipper A Great Year! - Teen Scrapbook, c. 1987.

1989

BARBIE® World of Fashion, c. 1988.

Skipper Teen Sister of BARBIE®, c. 1988.

1990

I'm into BARBIE®, c. 1990.

1991

BARBIE® Fashion and Fun™ Scrapbook, c. 1991.

1992

BARBIE® — She's got something special! Ready, set, go! with BARBIE® for Girls, c. 1991

1993

BARBIE® You've Got Something Special!

BARBIE® for Girls You've Got Something Special!, c.1992.

1994

BARBIE® Making Every Month Special!

BARBIE® for Girls Making Every Season Special!, c. 1993.

1996

Fashion Avenue™ Collection — Let's Go Shopping for BARBIE®, c. 1995.

1997

BARBIE® Fashion Avenue™ Collection, c. 1996.

These Fashion Booklets are in essence a miniature time-capsule of each year they represent. Today, the vast majority of these Fashion Booklets are hard to find.

147. ***The World of BARBIE® Fashions by Mattel***, c. 1966.

148. ***The World of BARBIE® Fashions by Mattel*** Book 1, 2 and 3, c. 1966.

149. ***The World of BARBIE® Fashions*** Book 1 and 2, c. 1967.

150. ***BARBIE®'sWorld: Bright, Swinging, Now.***, c. 1968.

151. ***The World of BARBIE® Fashions***, c.1968. One booklet was unnumbered; the other three were Book One (shown), Book Two and Book Three.

152. ***Living BARBIE® As full of life as you are.***, c. 1969, was available in 1970 included an advertising offer for the "New BARBIE® Fan Club".

153. ***Living BARBIE® and Living Skipper*** Booklets, c. 1970. Cover variations include: "Join the new BARBIE® Fan Club today!" (left) and "See letter from BARBIE® doll in back cover" (right).

154. ***The Lively World of BARBIE®***, c. 1971.

155. ***The Beautiful World of BARBIE®***, c.1972 and c.1973 featured the same cover.

156. Another Fashion Booklet was not available until 1977 when the ***World of BARBIE® Fashions***, c. 1976 appeared.

157. ***BARBIE® World of Fashions***, c. 1978.

158. ***BARBIE® World of Fashions***, c. 1979.

Chapter 8

FAMILY AND FRIENDS

BARBIE® doll has many family members and friends that play significant roles in her adventures. See page 124 for a Family Tree listing.

159. In 1963, a commercial advertised BARBIE® doll's new friend ***Midge®***, "with side glance eyes and teeth" (1963). Here she stands at the door of BARBIE® doll's Dream House wearing *Red Flare*. ***Allan™*** (1964) was her boyfriend. He wears the Ken® fashion, *Saturday Date* (1961-1963).

160. The book ***Portrait of Skipper (The Story of Skipper — A New doll)*** has illustrations of the Roberts' family — BARBIE®, Skipper and their parents. Published by Wonder Books, c. 1964.

161. ***Tutti*** and ***Todd*** dolls (1966) were BARBIE® doll's tiny twin sister and brother. Available in various issues from 1966-1970.

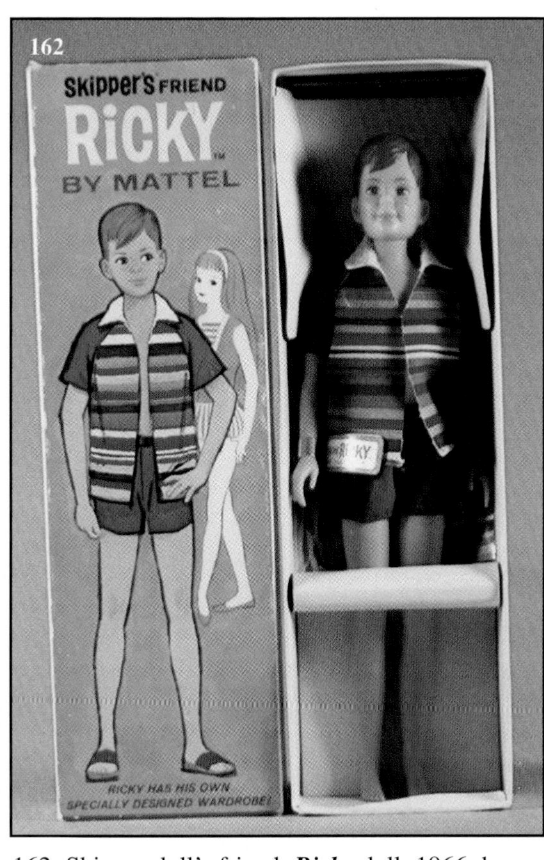

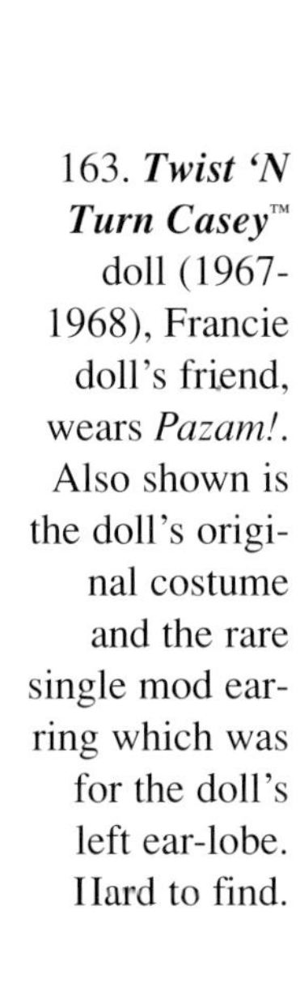

162. Skipper doll's friend, ***Ricky*** doll, 1966, has a pink 'skin-tone' plastic body. Rare.

163. ***Twist 'N Turn Casey***™ doll (1967-1968), Francie doll's friend, wears *Pazam!*. Also shown is the doll's original costume and the rare single mod ear-ring which was for the doll's left ear-lobe. Hard to find.

164. BARBIE® doll's Mod British chum ***Talking Stacey***™ was available from 1968-1970 in two basic issues. One was a Talking Stacey doll which spoke with a British dialect, 1968. Shown is ***Twist 'N Turn Stacey*** (1969) wearing *Togetherness*.

165. BARBIE® doll's MOD'ern cousin, ***Francie With Growin' Pretty Hair*** (1970). Very rare.

166. BARBIE® doll's friend, ***Walk Lively™ Steffie™*** (1972) could walk, whirl and twirl when placed on the

167. ***Growing Up™ Skipper*** (1975-1976) and friend ***Growing Up™ Ginger™*** (1976 only). Rare.

168. ***Super Teen™ Skipper*** (1979-1980) and ***Skipper's boyfriend Scott™*** (1980). Rare.

169. ***BARBIE® & Friends Gift Set*** (1983). The box stated that P.J. was BARBIE® doll's cousin up until the time of this gift set's release. Previous issues were referred to P.J. as BARBIE® doll's friend.

170. ***Sweet Roses***™ ***P.J.*** (1984) was the P.J. doll's finale. The character had been introduced in 1969 as BARBIE® doll's friend.

171. BARBIE® doll's friend, ***Tropical Miko***™ was introduced in 1986. Hard to Find. The Summer 1986 issue of *BARBIE® The Magazine for Girls* regular feature, "The BARBIE® Drama", says that Miko doll was from Akawaka Island and she was studying the Kula birds BARBIE® doll's Tropical Bird, Tahiti, (1986).

172. ***Tracy***®, bride (1983-1984) and ***Todd***™, groom (1983-1984) were BARBIE® doll's friends; shown with the ***Tracy & Todd Wedding Play Pak***.

173. ***Jewel Secrets***™ ***Whitney*** (c. 1986). Hard to Find.

174. ***Teen Dance Jazzie***™ (c.1988). Hard to Find This was the first issue of Jazzie doll, a teen cousin of BARBIE® doll.

175. ***Western Fun***™ ***Nia***™ (c. 1989) was BARBIE® doll's friend. ***Nia*** is an acronym for Native American. Rare.

176. The Wedding Party™ Midge Gift Set (1991) consists of six dolls, all very significant to BARBIE® doll's life. An announcement of BARBIE® doll's best friend Midge and Alan dolls "tying the knot" appeared in *People Magazine*.

177 A

Wedding Bells for Midge

177 A & B. Information on relatives and friends often comes from magazine articles like this one featured in *BARBIE® —The Magazine For Girls*, Summer 1991. The short story entitled "Wedding Bells for Midge" was written by Susan Brady and illustrated by Beverly Kirby. The story details Midge and Alan dolls' wedding plans and the wedding party members — Kelly BARBIE® doll's sister) as flower girl and Todd (Ken® doll's brother) as ring bearer.

178. ***Wedding Day™ Kelly & Todd Gift Set*** (1991) featured Kelly as the flower girl and Todd as the ring bearer. This gift set was a Toys R Us exclusive. Rare.

179. Ken® doll has been BARBIE® doll's boyfriend since 1961. Throughout the years they have participated in many weddings but have never tied the knot. Pictured here is ***Wedding Fantasy Gift Set*** (1994), a wholesale club exclusive. This gift set was recalled and then re-released to Kay-Bee Toy Stores. Rare.

180. Skipper doll's best friend Courtney have been available since 1989 in various issues. Shown are ***Phone Fun™ Skipper*** (1996) wearing *#15891 Skipper Fashion* (1996) and ***Phone Fun™ Courtney*** (1996) wearing *#14383 Skipper Fashion* (1996).

181. ***Winter Holiday BARBIE® Gift Set*** (1996) includes BARBIE® doll and her sisters, Skipper, Stacie, and Kelly dolls with their dog Koko.

182. ***Big Brother Ken®*** and ***Baby Brother Tommy™*** (1997).

Chapter 9

KEYS TO FAME — THE CAREERS

BARBIE® doll's many careers began in 1959 with a fashion model. Since that time, she has held many different positions, reflecting the changes in society. Ken® doll's careers have mirrored the changes in society as well. Both dolls have portrayed various professions.

183. ***BARBIE®'s Keys to Fame Game*** (1963) by Mattel, Inc. had players attempting to win fame in many different careers: astronaut, ballerina, movie star, nurse, stewardess, mother, fashion designer or teacher.

184. BARBIE® and Ken® dolls took to the skies. BARBIE® doll was an ***American Airlines Stewardess*** (1961-1964 fashion). Hard to Find. Ken® doll was an ***American Airlines Captain*** (1964- 1965 fashion). Rare. In 1973-1977 the duo would "fly the friendly skies" with United Airlines BARBIE® Friendship (see *Treasury of BARBIE® Doll Accessories* page 54 for more information).

185. ***#954 Career Girl*** (1963-1964). Hard to find.

186

186. BARBIE® doll sang the night away in ***#982 Solo In The Spotlight*** (1960-1964).

187. Fashions like ***#991 Registered Nurse*** (1961-1964) provided career changes for BARBIE®. Hard to find.

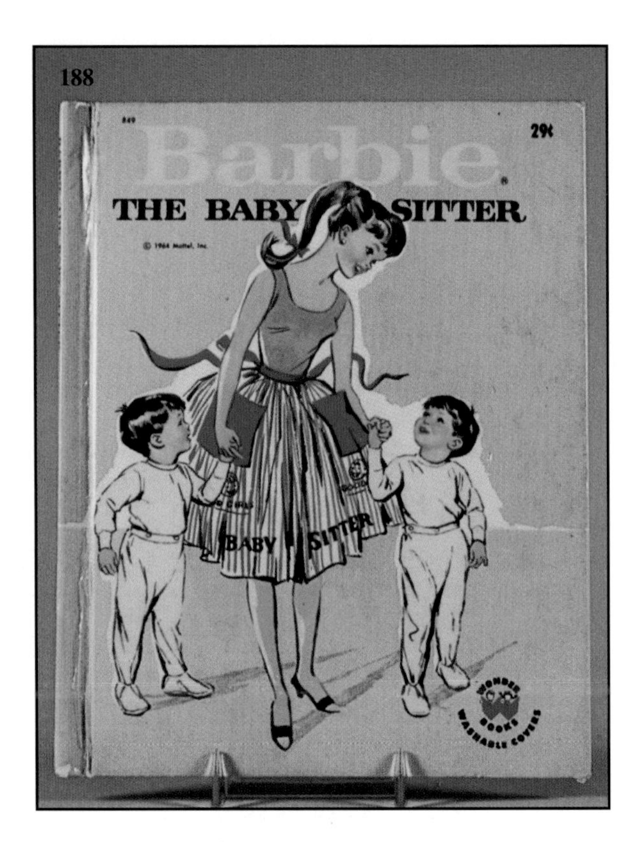

189. BARBIE® doll is known for her fashion style. This ***American Girl*** hair style doll with bendable legs (1965) wears *#1635 Fashion Editor* (1965). Hard to find. The fashion came complete with a camera. Rare.

188. ***BARBIE® The Baby Sitter***, c. 1964, was published under license by Wonder Books. This book's concept, as well as the cover art, is based on the fashion *#953 BARBIE® Baby-Sits*.

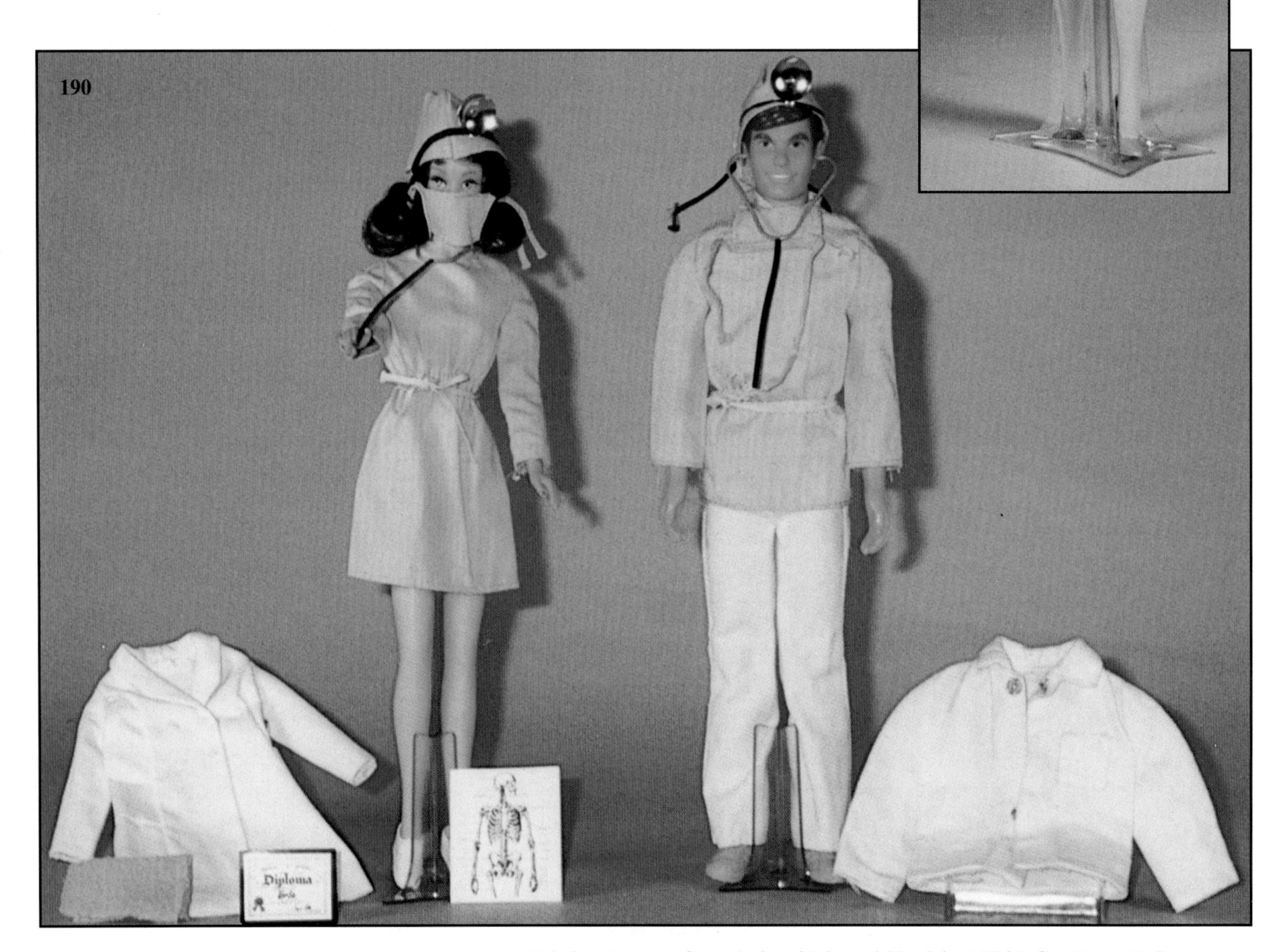

190. BARBIE® doll became a doctor in ***#7700 Get Ups 'N Go*** (1973- 1976) and Ken® in ***#7705 Get-Ups 'N Go*** (1973) became a surgeon. Both fashions are hard to find.

191. During the mid-'80s BARBIE® and Ken® dolls represented YUPPIES (a slang acronym for Young Urban Professionals). Pictured are ***Day-to-Night™ BARBIE®*** doll and ***Day-to-Night Ken®*** doll (1985-1986). BARBIE® doll wore a trendy pink ultra-suede-like suit with spectator pumps in white and pink. This is the only time BARBIE® doll has ever had spectator pumps.

192 & 193. ***Rappin' Rockin' BARBIE®*** (c.1991) had a book BARBIE® Rockin', Rappin', Dancin' World Tour Pop-Up Book to share her story. The book was published under license by Golden Book-Western Publishing Company, Inc. c. 1992. Hard to find.

194. This Mattel advertisement proclaimed BARBIE® as "The Doll Dreams Are Made Of". The ad featured ***Astronaut™ BARBIE®*** (1986). Hard to find.

195. The inside of ***BARBIE® Rockin', Rappin', Dancin', World Tour Pop-up Book***. The book was written by Staci Strong, illustrated by Pamela Duarte, designed by Doug Bergstreser, with paper engineering by Dennis K. Meyer. Hard to find.

196. ***Silver Screen BARBIE®*** (1994), a special limited edition for F.A.O. Schwarz, celebrated the golden age of film and the 1930s glamour.

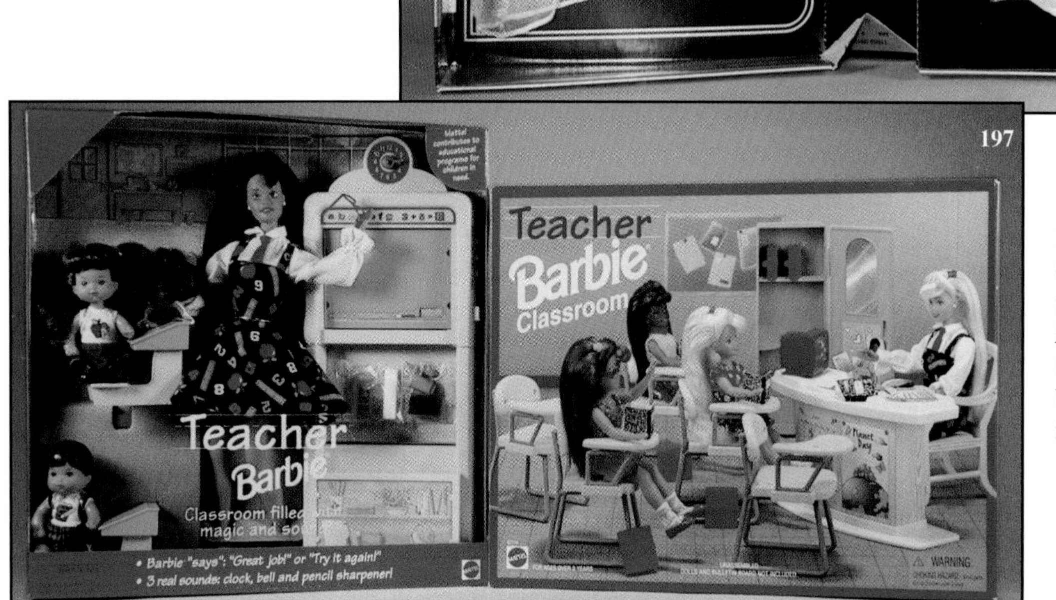

197. ***Teacher BARBIE® Gift Set***, Hispanic (1996) and the ***Teacher BARBIE® Classroom*** (1996). Both white and black dolls were available in 1995 and 1996.

198. ***Busy Gal™ BARBIE®*** (1995) wears a reproduction of *#981 Busy Gal* (1960-1961) fashion . This doll's advertisement is also illustrated.

199. In 1996 BARBIE® doll was a veterinarian ***Pet Doctor BARBIE®*** (1996). She even had a ***Pet Doctor BARBIE® Check Up and Play Center*** (1996).

200. BARBIE® and Ken® dolls have successful careers and money in the bank with ***BARBIE® So Much To Do!™ Bank*** (1996). BARBIE® doll is wearing *#14980 Fashion Avenue* (1996). Ken® doll is wearing *#13567 Fashion Avenue* (1996) and Skipper doll is wearing *#14383 Skipper Fashion* (1996).

Chapter 10

"...And Now A Word From Our Sponsor"

Television commercials were aired as early as 1948. Each commercial was introduced by a broadcast announcer with the words "...and now a word from our Sponsor." Mattel, Inc. was the first toy company to advertise on television in 1955 as a segment sponsor of "The Mickey Mouse Club".

Throughout the years, television commercials, brand-name merchandise, and BARBIE® doll items have captured the traditions and culture of American society. The timeliness of BARBIE® doll and her many accessories has even been paired with popular merchandise as you will see here. "...and Now a Word from our sponsor."

201. ***Angel Face™ BARBIE®*** (1983) came with her own makeup — two eyeshadows and blusher in a carrying case. "Angel Face" was a trademark of Cheesbrough-Ponds, Inc. used with permission. This doll was featured on the cover of *BARBIE® — The Magazine for Girls*, premier issue Winter 1984.

202. BARBIE®, Ken® and Skipper dolls enjoy working behind the counter at the ***BARBIE® Loves McDonald®'s Restaurant*** (1983-1984). Hard to find complete. The dolls are wearing authentic McDonald's costumes designed by Mattel's Janet Goldblatt. Each fashion is entitled *Fun at McDonald's*. Hard to find.

203. ***Pepsi™ Spirit BARBIE®*** (c.1989), rare and ***Pepsi Spirit Skipper*** (c.1989), rare. Mattel, Inc. used the Pepsi-Cola registered trademark under license for these Toys R Us exclusives.

204. ***Ice Capades 50th Anniversary - BARBIE® Pendant***. The theme of the 1989 Ice Capades tour was the "Exclusive Live Tour of BARBIE®".

205. ***United Colors of Benetton BARBIE®*** (1990). Benetton was an international clothing manufacturer. The doll was available through catalogues and Benetton retail stores. Also available were Ken® doll (except in the U.S.), Teresa doll (except in the U.S.), Christie doll, and Marina doll (named Kira in the U.S.).

206. ***All-American BARBIE®*** and ***All-American Ken®*** dolls (1990). Each doll came with Reebok footwear.

207. ***BARBIE® Flintstones Funwear Gift Set*** (c. 1994) was manufactured by Arcotoys, Inc., a Mattel Company.

208. ***Happy Meal® Stacie*** and twin brother ***Happy Meal Todd*** dolls (c. 1993). The McDonald's Corporation trademarks were used for the Happy Meal Box. The Golden Arches logo was used on the design of their shirts.

209. With the permission of the Ford Motor Company, Mattel issued a ***BARBIE® Mustang™*** (1995). The car magically expands from a two to four seater! (Four seater shown.) Hard to find. BARBIE® Me and My Mustang™! doll (shown) (1995) was a wholesale shopping club exclusive. Hard to find.

210. Here is the BARBIE® Mustang as a two seater with BARBIE® Me and My Mustang doll waving the pink slip of ownership.

211. These three sets of realistic pretend food items display brand names found on 1996 grocery shelves. They are: ***BARBIE® Fun Fixin'™ Cake Set, BARBIE® Fun Fixin'™ Barbecue Set,*** and ***BARBIE® Fun Fixin'™ Dinner Set.***

212. BARBIE® doll makes a cake with miniatures: Duncan Hines Moist Deluxe Cake Mix and Duncan Hines Creamy Homestyle Frosting. Both miniatures were included in the ***BARBIE® Fun Fixin'™ Cake Set*** (c. 1995). This set was limited in availability at the time of issue and predicted to be hard to find in the future due to small pieces.

213. After playing ball, BARBIE® and Ken® dolls are ready for a barbeque with ***BARBIE® Fun Fixin™ Barbeque Set*** (c.1995). The set came complete with hot dogs and hamburgers, miniature bottles of Gulden's Spicy Brown Mustard and Del Monte Ketchup and other all-American food. This set was limited in availability at the time of issue and predicted to be hard to find in the future due to numerous small pieces.

214. BARBIE® doll is preparing a special dinner with all the trimmings — Ocean Spray jellied cranberry sauce, Birds-Eye sliced carrots and Pepperidge Farm Country Style Classic dinner rolls. ***BARBIE® Fun Fixin™ Dinner Set*** (c. 1995) includes many small pieces, one of which is a turkey baster. This set was limited in availability at the time of issue and predicted to be hard to find in the future due to small pieces.

215. ***BARBIE® So Much To Do!™ — Cleanin' House*** (c.1995) has four miniature household products: Lemon Pledge furniture polish, Pine-Sol cleaner, Formula 409 and Easy-On Speed starch. BARBIE® doll has her choice of houses to clean (see *Treasury of BARBIE® Doll Accessories* pages 31-35).

216. ***BARBIE® Lee™ Jeans Fashions*** (c. 1995).

217. The 1995 Mattel catalogue did not list, nor illustrate ***Pizza Party! Skipper's Pizza Shop***. It is hard to find as it was not available in all BARBIE® doll isles and limited to one year only. This item was copyrighted 1994 and is a Pizza Hut, Inc. restaurant registered trademark of PepsiCo., Inc.

218. ***Got Milk?™ BARBIE®*** (1996, Toys R Us exclusive).

"Got Milk?" is a registered trademark of the California Milk Processor Board.

219. ***Soda Fountain Sweetheart™ BARBIE®*** (c. 1996) is the first in the Coca-Cola® Fashion Classic Series. Also shown: The 1996 Holiday Coca-Cola Catalog featuring this BARBIE® doll on its cover.

220. ***Cool Shavin'™ Ken®*** (1996) came with a pretend bottle of "Old Spice After Shave". Mattel, Inc. used this trademark of Shulton, Inc. with permission.

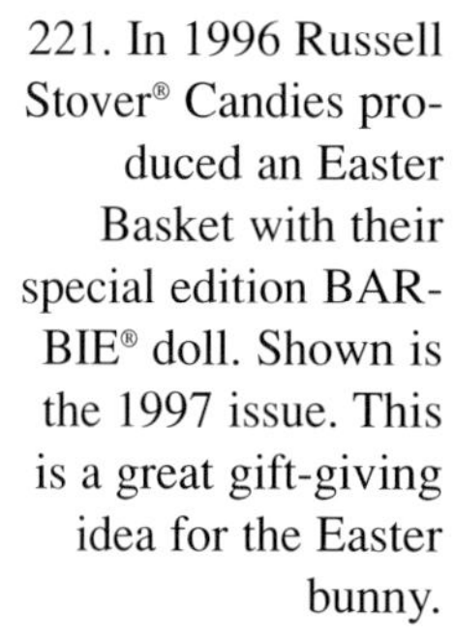

221. In 1996 Russell Stover® Candies produced an Easter Basket with their special edition BARBIE® doll. Shown is the 1997 issue. This is a great gift-giving idea for the Easter bunny.

Chapter 11

Mattel, Inc. and the Walt Disney Company

In 1955 Mattel hired ad agency Carson/Roberts to promote their toys. Carson/Roberts suggested an unprecedented idea (at the time). Mattel would become a segment sponsor of a new show titled, "The Mickey Mouse Club". The show was produced by Walt Disney and aired Monday through Friday at 5.00 p.m. on the ABC television network. Seventy-five percent of T.V. viewers between 1955 and 1959 were tuned into "The Mickey Mouse Club" which gave Mattel, Inc. excellent exposure for their toys.

In 1988, 29 years later, Mattel, Inc. and The Walt Disney Company began another toy relationship including the production of Disney film characters. In 1990, 35 years after Mattel, Inc. sponsored, "The Mickey Mouse Club", BARBIE® doll received her "mouse ears". The doll was a Child World/Children's Palace exclusive called "Mattel-Disney BARBIE®". A Toys R Us exclusive called "BARBIE® & Friends Gift Set - Dressin' Up with Mickey, Minnie, & Donald" followed in 1991. A special theme park exclusive for Disneyland® Paris near Paris, France, called "Disney Weekend BARBIE®" appeared in 1993. Later that same year a new show called, "The Magical World of BARBIE®", sponsored by Mattel, Inc., premiered in Epcot at The Walt Disney World Resort in Florida. Exclusive Walt Disney Theme Park dolls include the following:

Disney Fun BARBIE® (1993)
Disney Fun BARBIE®, 2nd Edition (1994)
Disney Fun BARBIE®, 3rd Edition (1995)
Disney Fun BARBIE®, 4th Edition
Mickey's Toontown™ Stacie (1994)
Walt Disney World BARBIE® (1996)

Mattel, Inc. and The Walt Disney Company have brought fun memories to children and the young at heart.

222. ***Disney Weekend BARBIE®*** (c. 1993), wearing Mickey Mouse ears, was an exclusive for Disneyland® Paris. Hard to find.
Disney characters © Disney Enterprises, Inc.
Used by permission from Disney Enterprises, Inc.

223. The Child World/Children's Palace toy retailer exclusive was this ***Mattel - Disney BARBIE®*** doll (1990). Rare.
Disney characters © Disney Enterprises, Inc.
Used by permission from Disney Enterprises, Inc.

224. ***Disney Fun*™ *BAR-BIE*®** (1993). This doll was the first in the series, as well as the first exclusive BARBIE® doll for Walt Disney Theme Parks and Resorts.

225. ***Disney Fun*™ *BARBIE*®**, second edition (1994) exclusive for Walt Disney Theme Parks and Resorts.

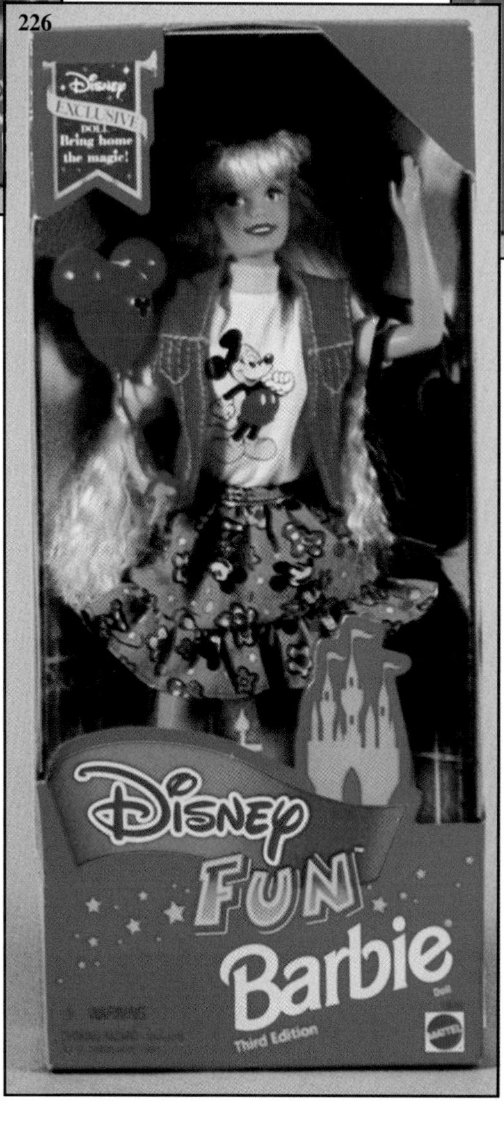

226. ***Disney Fun*™ *BARBIE*®**, third edition (c.1995) was an exclusive for Walt Disney Theme Parks and Resorts.

227. What better way to celebrate your 25th anniversary of Walt Disney World® Resort than with a BARBIE® doll exclusive, ***Walt Disney World BARBIE***® (c.1996).

228. ***Mickey's Toontown***™ ***Stacie*** (1994), the littlest sister of BARBIE® doll, was an exclusive for Walt Disney Theme Parks and Resorts.

229. This menagerie of dolls includes ***Native American BARBIE***® dolls as well as the ***American Indian BARBIE***® doll with a papoose. They are shown with the Disney Pocahontas Powhatan Village Playset (1995).

230. ***Disney's 101 Dalmations Basket O' Puppies*** was released in late 1996.
Disney characters © Disney Enterprises, Inc.
Used by permission from Disney Enterprises, Inc.

231. ***BARBIE***® ***& Friends Gift Set — Dressin' up with Mickey, Minnie, & Donald*** (c.1991) was a Toys R Us exclusive. Rare. BARBIE®, Ken®, and Skipper dolls each have Mickey Mouse ears and Disney character shirts copyrighted by The Walt Disney Company.
Disney characters © Disney Enterprises, Inc.
Used by permission from Disney Enterprises, Inc.

Chapter 12

MATTEL, INC. AND THE TRADITIONS OF THE OLYMPICS

BARBIE® doll represents a historical Olympic heritage for two very important reasons: Mattel's sponsoring of the event and her representation of the aspirations of hopeful Olympic athletes. In 1975 and 1976, Mattel had a $2-million advertising promotion which was authorized by the United States Olympic Committee. Dolls, accessories and fashions such as the following were produced:

Gold Medal™ BARBIE® represented a United States Olympic swimmer.

Gold Medal™ BARBIE® and her Olympic wardrobe, a Sears exclusive. Her U.S. Olympic wardrobe consisted of three complete outfits: Olympic parade dress, swimsuit and ice-skating costume.

Gold Medal™ BARBIE® Skater represented a United States Olympic skater.

Gold Medal™ BARBIE® Winter Sports consisted of two fashions: a U.S. Olympic skier outfit and an after-skiing fashion.

Gold Medal™ BARBIE® Skier represented a U.S. skier.

Gold Medal™ Ken® Skier represented a U.S. skier.

Gold Medal™ P.J. Gymnast represented a U.S. gymnast.

The accessories were as follows:

Olympic Gymnast Set for BARBIE® and P.J.

BARBIE® Olympic Ski Village

The fashions were as follows:

BARBIE® Get-Ups 'N Go — #7243 Olympic Warm-Ups

BARBIE® Get-Ups 'N Go — #7244 Olympic Parade

BARBIE® Best Buy — #7271/#7413 Olympic Outfit

BARBIE® Best Buy — #7272 Olympic Skating

Ken® Get-Ups 'N Go — #7247 Olympic Hockey

Skipper Get-Ups 'N Go — #7251 Olympic Skating

232. The Modern Olympic games celebrated the centennial anniversary in 1996. BARBIE® doll has represented the aspirations of hopeful Olympic athletes as a result of Mattel, Inc. sponsoring various Olympic games throughout the years.

233. BARBIE® doll wears ***Get-Ups 'N Go — Olympic Parade***" (1975). Hard to find.

Skipper Best Buy — #7274 Olympic Swimsuit
Francie Best Buy — #7273 Olympic Outfit

Some international BARBIE® dolls were also produced. They are as follows:

BARBIE® Olympia in a red, white and blue swimsuit was available for Italy in 1976.

Skating Star BARBIE® represents a Canadian ice skater. She was produced in 1988 for the winter games in Calgary, Canada.

Mattel, Inc. produced three dolls as official licensed products of The Atlanta Committee for the Olympic Games, Inc for the centennial anniversary of the Olympic Games. These dolls were available in 1996 and listed as follows:

Olympic Gymnast BARBIE® (blonde)
Olympic Gymnast BARBIE® (African-American)
Olympic Gymnast BARBIE® (auburn, Toys R Us Exclusive)

234. ***BARBIE® Olympic Ski Village*** (1975).

235. ***Gold Medal BARBIE***® (1975). The doll came with a Miniature Olympic Gold Medal and a child-size Olympic patch. Skipper doll wears *#7274 Best Buy — Olympic Swimsuit* (1975). This fashion also came with a miniature Gold Medal and a terry cloth towel in red, white and blue.

236. ***Olympic Gymnast Set for BARBIE® and P.J.*** (1974). Hard to find. Mattel, Inc. was authorized to manufacture this item by the U.S. Olympic Committee.

237. ***Olympic Gymnast BARBIE***® (1996), an official licensed product of the Atlanta Committee for the Olympic Games, Inc. This doll with auburn hair was a Toys R Us exclusive. The blonde and African-American versions were distributed to various toy retailers.

238. Mattel's ***BARBIE® Dolls of the World and Mattel Hot Wheels® —McDonald's Happy Meal™ Display*** (1996) featured an Olympic theme. Hard to find. McDonald's was a sponsor and the official restaurant of the 1996 Olympic Games. On the right, ***Olympic Gymnast BARBIE® — Blonde*** (1996). Mattel, Inc. was also a sponsor of the 1996 Summer Olympic Games.

239. ***McDonald's Canadian BARBIE® Olympic Gymnast Figurine*** (1996). This figurine was for the McDonald's Corp. Happy Meals in Canada. Hard to find.

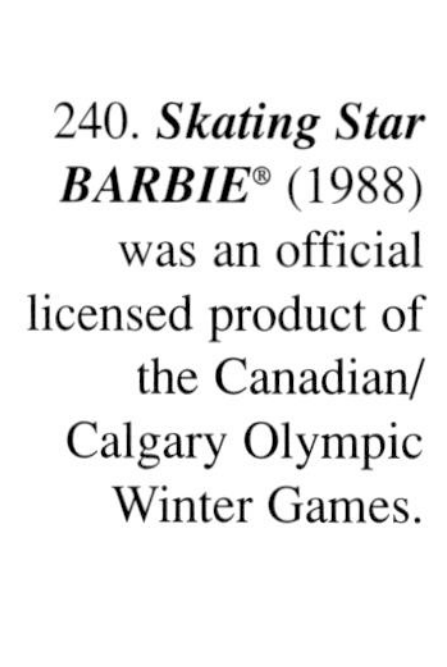

240. ***Skating Star BARBIE®*** (1988) was an official licensed product of the Canadian/ Calgary Olympic Winter Games.

Chapter 13

Hooray for the Red, White, and Blue!

BARBIE® doll, family and friends have mirrored the thoughts, views and special times of our country. In 1976, the U.S. celebrated its bicentennial and BARBIE® doll was there to celebrate. Mattel produced special fashions for BARBIE®, Ken® and Skipper dolls to share in the festivities.

To capture the pride of the U.S. Armed Service, Mattel began a military series in 1989. Cooperation from each branch of the armed forces to make the costumes as accurate as possible was received. According to a 1990 article in *The Washington Post* prototypes underwent Pentagon procurements to comply with military regulations. The military series 'marched' right into collectibility with dolls representing the Army, Air Force, Navy, and Marine Corps.

BARBIE® doll continues to represent the patriotic and proud image that Americans hold for their country. Hooray for the red, white, and blue!

241. The U.S. has multitudinous symbols of freedom. In 1976, the nation celebrated its bicentennial; to commemorate Mattel produced special fashions for BARBIE®, Ken® and Skipper dolls. Shown here are ***Ken® — #9132 Best Buy***, ***Skipper — Get Ups 'N Go #9165, Bicentennial Fashion Patriotic & Pretty***, and ***BARBIE® — Best Buy #9158 Bicentennial Dress***. Rare.

242. ***Army BARBIE***® (1989) represented the military as a captain. She is dressed in authentic officer's evening uniform. Also illustrated is the "Mattel, Inc. 1989 Collector Classics Catalogue" showing this doll.

243
Barbie Salutes Our Country's Armed Forces

243. BARBIE® Salutes Our Country's Armed Forces 1990 advertisement for ***Navy BARBIE***® and ***Air Force BARBIE***®.

244. ***Navy BARBIE***® (c.1990) was second in the Stars 'N Stripes™ Series. Wearing the official U.S. Navy uniform for enlisted women, BARBIE® doll represents a Petty Officer.

245. ***Air Force BARBIE***® (c.1990) was third in Stars 'N Stripes™ Series. Wearing a flight-suit and jacket with authentic A-2 insignia which is issued to mission qualified aircrew members, BARBIE® doll represents a Captain.

246. The Stars 'N Stripes™ Series, ***Marine Corps BARBIE® & Ken® Deluxe Set*** (c. 1991) are dressed in authentic "dress blues" uniforms for enlisted personal. Each has the rank of Sergeant.

247. ***Army BARBIE® & Ken® Deluxe Set*** (c. 1992) of the Stars 'N Stripes™ Series. These dolls represent the enlisted Desert Storm personnel of the 101st Airborne division from Fort Campbell, Kentucky. BARBIE® doll was a medic, ranking a Sergeant. Ken® doll was Staff Sergeant wearing the unit's insignia "Rendezvous With Destiny" on his beret.

248. The Stars 'N Stripes™ Series, ***Air Force BARBIE® & Ken® Deluxe Set*** (c.1993). BARBIE® doll's rank is Lt. Col. while Ken® doll is a Captain in the Air Force Thunderbirds.

249. This advertisement explains that Mattel, Inc. donated 37¢ of the cost of the doll to the United States Committee for UNICEF to help children in 121 countries. ***UNICEF BARBIE®*** (c. 1989) wears a flowing blue gown with stars, white bodice and red sash, the same colors as the U.S. flag.

250. BARBIE® For President (c.1991) came with a campaign button for the individual. This doll was a Toys R Us exclusive. A rare version has the presidential seal of the United States.

251. BARBIE® doll celebrated the 25th anniversary of the Apollo 11 moonwalk in 1994 with the Toys R Us exclusive ***Astronaut BARBIE®*** (1994). Her ensemble included glow-in-the-dark moon rocks, authentic look NASA (logo used with permission) space helmet and spacesuit.

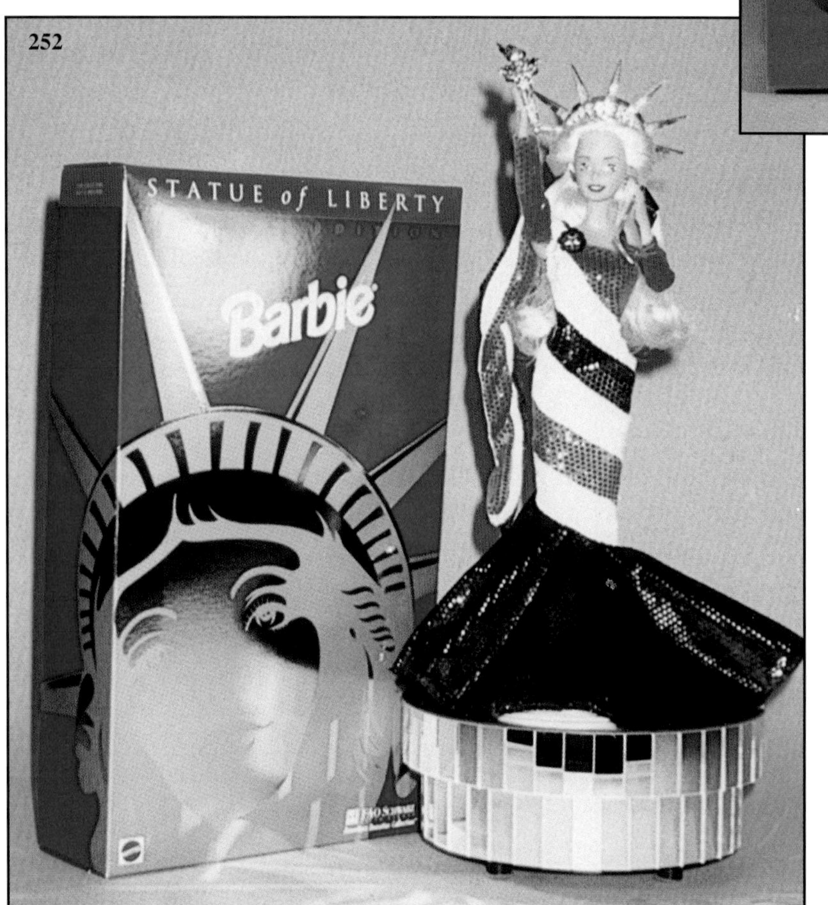

252. The F.A.O. Schwarz exclusive, ***Statue of Liberty BARBIE®*** (1996) commemorated the 110th anniversary of the Statue of Liberty. This is the first doll in the American Beauties Collection.

Chapter 14

INNOVATIONS

Technological advancements have shaped and molded the evolution of dolls from the early days through current time. No one knows what the future may hold, but with BARBIE®, family, friends, accessories and fashions we will discover a new world together.

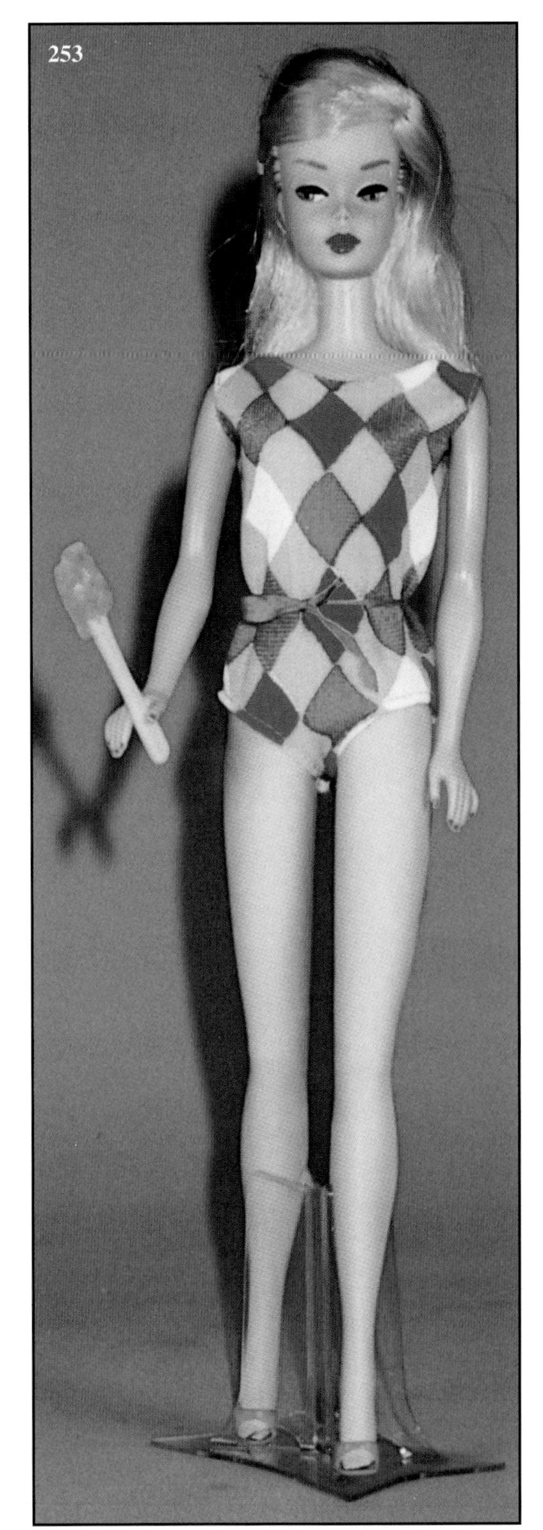

253. ***Color Magic BARBIE***® (1966-1967) was issued with golden hair as shown. Her hair could be changed to scarlet with a sponge applicator This doll was also available with midnight-black hair which could be changed to ruby. The doll's swimsuit could also change in color. Rare.

254. Francie™ doll (1966) was the first doll to have rooted eyelashes! In 1967, BARBIE® dolls were issued with rooted eyelashes. Several other dolls would follow this suit. Illustrated is a ***Twist 'N Turn BARBIE***® doll wearing *Winter Wedding* (1969-1970). Rare.

255. BARBIE® doll and friends talked (1968-1969) when a pull-string on the back of their necks was pulled. (Left to right) ***Talking P.J.*** wears *Knit hit;* ***Talking Stacey***, who talked with a British dialect, wears *Snap -Dash*; ***Talking Ken***® wears *Big Business* and ***Talking BARBIE***® wears *All That Jazz.*

257. Magic Moves BARBIE® (1985) has movable arms. All that is required is a push of the switch located on the doll's back.

256. ***Western BARBIE***® (1981-1982) winked her left eye when a panel was pressed on her back. A few years after issue, these dolls no longer winked and the molded lashes have sunk back within the head.

258. ***BARBIE® Porsche 911 Cabriolet*** (c.1992). This sports car has real working headlights! It requires two "C" alkaline batteries. Hard to find.

259. ***Sparkle Eyes***™ ***BARBIE***® (1992) and ***Sparkle Surprise Ken***® (1992). Rhinestones made the doll's eyes sparkle. The magenta sports-car is the ***Porsche 911 Cabriolet*** with real working headlights.

260. ***Teen Talk!***™ ***BARBIE***® (1992) was available in three different hair colors: blonde, red and brown (shown). Each doll required three alkaline watch batteries and said four phrases. This doll made the news when some said "Math class is tough".

261. ***Angel Lights***™ ***BARBIE***® (c.1993) was electrical with 20 flickering lights. This doll was designed to be a treetop or centerpiece.

262. ***Twinkle Lights BARBIE***® (c.1993) came with two "N" size alkaline batteries to enable the twinkling. When BARBIE® doll's belt was turned, Twinkle Optics™ shimmer in three colors: white, blue, and pink. This doll had a Patent Pending. Rare. The greeting card (on right) was a Hallmark Cards, Inc. "Happy Birthday" card made under license from Mattel, Inc. (c.1994).

263. ***BARBIE***® ***2-in-1 Porch Swing & Grill*** (c.1993) was made in Italy for global distribution. The parakeet on the left sings. It requires two LR44 batteries. Rare.

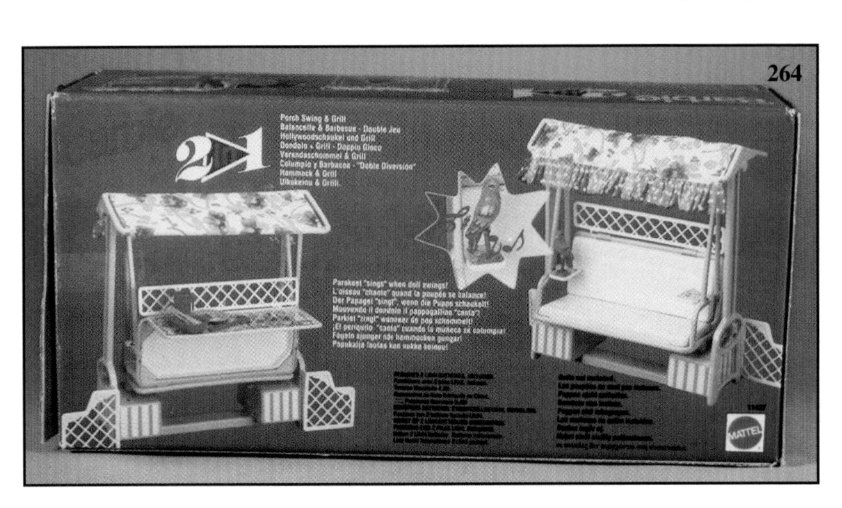

264. The box shows the features of the ***BARBIE***® ***2-in-1 Porch Swing & Grill***.

265. These BARBIE® doll pets have realistic features. ***BARBIE® High Stepper™ Horse*** (c.1994) requires four "AA" alkaline batteries to walk. ***Puppy Ruff™*** (c.1994) barks and ***Mitzi Meow™*** (c.1994) meows. Both require three AG-13 button cell alkaline batteries.

266. ***BARBIE® Talking Colorforms™*** (c.1994) was manufactured under license from Mattel by Colorforms Brand. It has the Colorforms™ Brand play surface for use with the vinyl play pieces. The board makes sounds when one of the ten pink dots are pressed. The sounds include: a ringing telephone, the tick-tock of the clock, a cat's meowing and seagulls calling. Three batteries, No. LR44/G13/357, are required for activation of sound. Hard to find.

267. ***Dance n' Twirl™ BARBIE®*** (1994) was the first BARBIE® doll ever to dance by radio control!

268. ***BARBIE® Enchanted Evening, 1960 Nightlight*** (c. 1994) has an on/off switch. This item is from the 'From BARBIE® With Love' line made under license by Enesco Corporation. Requires a 7 Watt, type C7 bulb. Available for a short time. Rare.

269. ***BARBIE® and Ken® Senior Prom, 1963 musical*** (c. 1994) plays the tune "Notre Dame Victory March". This item is from the "From BARBIE® With Love" line produced under license by Enesco Corporation. This very unique porcelain musical features a ponytail BARBIE® doll wearing *#951 Senior Prom* and a Ken® doll wearing *#770 Campus Hero*. Both are riding in the BARBIE® Austin Healy Sports Car.

270. ***BARBIE® Boutique*** (1995) was made in Italy and available at U. S. toy stores with global distribution. The lights flash, doors open, music plays — all with three "C" alkaline batteries. As stated on the box, it is "Super Cool, echt schick! BARBIE® Boutique and Café!" (It's the coolest boutique and café in town).

271. ***Super Talk!™ BARBIE®*** (c. 1995) requires four AG-13 alkaline batteries. The doll to say over 100,000 different things. Example: "Cool! You could get ice-cream with our group".

272. ***Ocean Friends™ BARBIE® and Keiko Gift Set*** (1996). With assistance Keiko swims, splashes, squirts water and when gently squeezed will make whale sounds. Keiko is the real-life name of the orca whale in the film "Free Willy". Mattel, Inc. donated $500,000 to the Free Willy-Keiko Foundation from the Ocean Friends™ BARBIE® doll line.

273. ***BARBIE®, Leader of the Pack Motorcycle*** (1996) was a luncheon souvenir at the "BARBIE® and the Bandstand" National BARBIE® Doll Convention held in Philadelphia, PA. The motorcycle headlights and tail-lights work. The cycle also makes motorcycle noises when the "press here" button is pressed.

Chapter 15

BARBIE® DOLL'S DESIGNER LABEL WARDROBE

BARBIE® doll has always dressed to the nines in a spectacular wardrobe. Her famous model look has been achieved by in-house designers as well as famous fashion designers.

It all began in 1957 when Mattel, Inc. hired Charlotte Johnson to design a wardrobe for the yet-to-be released 11-1/2 inch fashion model BARBIE® doll. Johnson, a former women's clothing designer, designed innumerable garments. Her initials "C.J." appear on the packages of the 1975 BARBIE® doll Fashion Originals.

Oscar de' la Renta was the first fashion designer in the U.S. to have a designer signature on BARBIE® doll's wardrobe. "Entertainment Tonight" broadcasted the debut of these fashions (From the Collection of Oscar de' la Renta for BARBIE®) at a special black tie Mattel event held at the Waldorf Astoria in New York, February 12th, 1985. Life-size versions of BARBIE® doll's fashions were modeled by the then Miss America, Suzette Charles; actress Rebecca Holden, the daughter of actor, William Holden; Genie Francis, best known as "Laura" of the daytime drama, *General Hospital* and Cathy Lee Crosby, spokesperson/ model/actress. Each BARBIE® fashion had a special label stating the designer logo and identifying that fashion as part of the collector series. Later in the year, Mattel, Inc. held a showcase entitled, "Mighty Toy Explorama" to make Oscar de' la Renta's design of the "Peaches 'N Cream BARBIE® doll costume public. Oscar de' la Renta does not receive name credit on the package. In 1986, the series had five new editions.

Then in 1990 Mattel created a new division called, "Timeless Creations, the Collectible/ Specialty Doll Division of Mattel, Inc." This divi-

274. Charlotte Johnson designed BARBIE® doll fashions from 1957 to 1980. Her initials "C.J." appear on the packages of the BARBIE® doll Fashion Originals. The three shown fashions are: ***#7931 Red Velvet Evening Cape*** (1975), ***#7932 Metallic and Red Velvet Gown*** (1975), ***#7934 Pink Azalea Colored Gown*** (1975).

275. ***Peaches 'N Cream BARBIE®*** (1985-1986). Her chiffon gown and stole were designed by Oscar de' la Renta. His name was not mentioned on the box, although the news was made public in 1985 at a Mattel showcase entitled, "Mighty Toy Explorama". Very hard to find.

276. This red gown is ***Oscar de' la Renta Collector Series IV*** (1985). Hard to find. A life-size version of this fashion was modeled by Suzette Charles.

sion produced excellent quality, special and/or limited edition dolls for the collector. The first doll was a Bob Mackie BARBIE® doll, 5405-9992 (later known as Gold Sequin Bob Mackie BARBIE®).

Bob Mackie is a very talented multi-faceted Hollywood film, television and Broadway stage costume designer. His clientel has included: Judy Garland, Carol Burnett, Bette Midler, Diana Ross, and others. This special series of BARBIE® dolls consists of nine dolls. The series ran for seven years (1990-1996) and included the following:

Gold Sequin Bob Mackie BARBIE® 5405-9992, c. 1990
Starlight Splendor® BARBIE®, c. 1991
Platinum® BARBIE®, c. 1991
Neptune Fantasy® BARBIE®, c. 1992
Empress Bride® BARBIE®, c. 1992
Masquerade Ball® BARBIE®, c. 1993
Queen of Hearts® BARBIE®, c. 1994
Goddess of The Sun® BARBIE®, c. 1995
Moon Goddess® BARBIE®, c. 1996

In 1992, Mattel, Inc. began their own in-house designer series called the "Classique® Collection", showcasing the artists who create BARBIE® doll's wardrobe. Another collection, The Presidential Porcelain Barbie Collection™ features exquisitely dressed dolls like Royal Splendor, whose violet-purple satin gown has approximately 62,000 hand embroidered stitches.

Special dolls were also produced as store exclusives. Bloomingdales began a special store designer series in 1994. Each designer highlighted their signature style in the doll's costuming.

Mattel, Inc. has always kept BARBIE® doll fashionable. Planned creations include those by Ralph Lauren, Bill Blass, Christian Dior, Bob Mackie and Annie Klein.

277. This teal and royal blue brocade gown with royal blue taffeta cape is ***Oscar de' la Renta Collector Series V*** (1985). Hard to find. A life-size version of this fashion was modeled by Rebecca Holden, daughter of actor William Holden.

278. This fuchsia and gold print lamé with cape is ***Oscar de' la Renta Collectors Series VI*** (1985). Hard to find. A life-size version of this fashion was modeled by Genie Francis

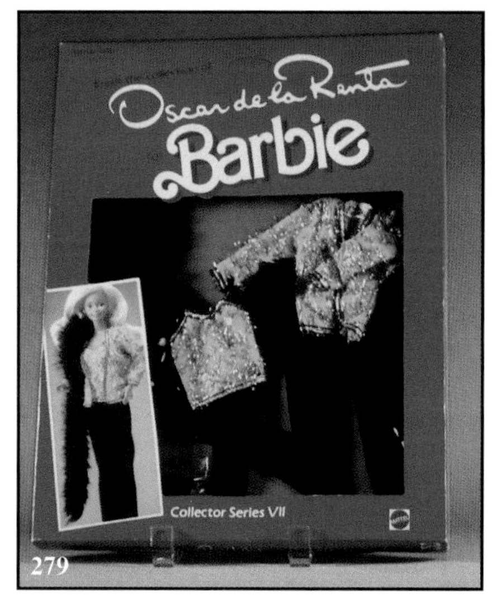

279. This gold and black ensemble featuring slacks and a long skirt is ***Oscar de' la Renta Collector Series VII*** (1985). Hard to find. A life-size version of this fashion was modeled by Cathy Lee Crosby.

280. This taffeta royal blue gown with matching boa is ***Oscar de' la Renta Collector Series VIII*** (1986). Very, very rare. This fashion was not distributed to all regions of the U.S.

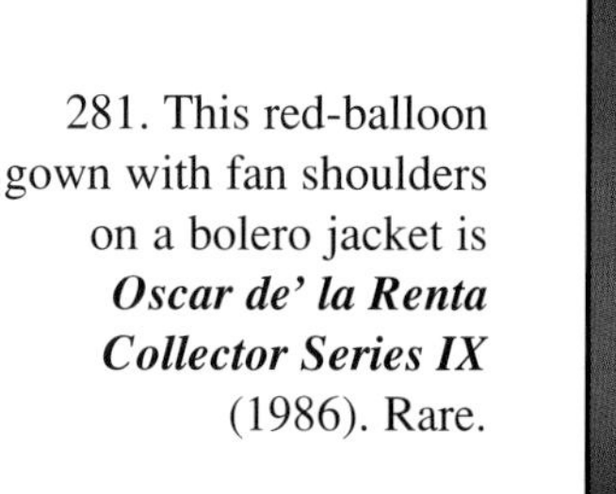
281. This red-balloon gown with fan shoulders on a bolero jacket is ***Oscar de' la Renta Collector Series IX*** (1986). Rare.

282. This fuchsia and violet velvet gown with bolero jacket is ***Oscar de' la Renta Collector Series X*** (1986). Rare.

283. This fuchsia evening dress changes into an evening gown. ***Oscar de' la Renta Collector Series XI*** (1986). Rare.

284. This two-piece royal blue gown is ***Oscar de' la Renta Collector Series XII*** (1986). Rare.

285. ***Gold Sequin Bob Mackie BARBIE®,*** 5405-9992 (c.1990) was the first in the series. This doll does not have a specific name as the other eight in series, but is often referred to as the "Gold Sequin BARBIE®"doll. This doll did not come in a multi-color box but did come with the shipping carton as seen in the foreground with packing materials to protect the display case. Gold Sequin BARBIE® doll is the only doll to come with a display case! Also shown is a replica of the original sketch.

286. ***Starlight Splendor™ BARBIE®*** (c.1991) was second in the Bob Mackie series. The replica of the original sketch includes the dramatic headdress, glitz of the gown's five thousand hand-sewn sequins and beads, and the flourish of feathers.

287. ***Platinum™ BARBIE®*** (c.1991), third in the Bob Mackie series, has a replica of the original sketch. The sketch includes the platinum hair and specially designed jewelry of this 8,000 hand-sewn bugle beads and pearlescent sequins masterpiece.

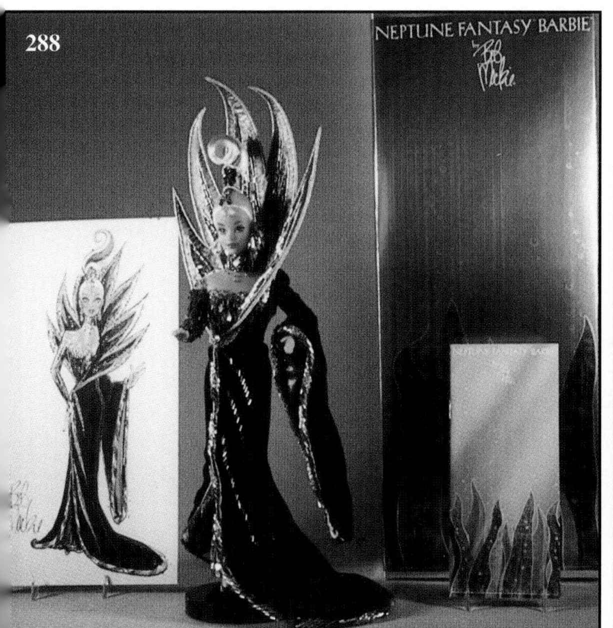

288. ***Neptune Fantasy*® *BARBIE*®** (c.1992) was fourth in the Bob Mackie series. The replica of the original sketch includes every detail from the teal highlight in the platinum up-swept hair style to the teal velvet coat lining in a metallic teal fabric.

289. ***Empress Bride*® *BARBIE*®** (c.1992) was fifth in the Bob Mackie series. This replica of the original sketch has a front and a side-view of this beautiful wedding gown.

290. The Classique Collection by Mattel designers began in 1992. First in the series was ***Benefit Ball*® *BARBIE*®** doll wearing a teal and gold lame gown designed by Carol Spencer. On the right is a certified signature document that certifies the item has been personally numbered and autographed by the designer.

291. In 1992, two Classique fashions designed by Mattel's Carol Spencer were available separately. These fashions were ***BARBIE*® *Hollywood Premiere*™** and ***BARBIE*® *Fifth Avenue Style*™**. Both are hard to find. The boxes were illustrated with copies of the designer's sketches. These two boxes were personally signed by the designer, although, all were not.

292. BARBIE® Hollywood Premiere™ (1992).

293. BARBIE® Fifth Avenue Style™ (1992).

294. ***Masquerade Ball™ BARBIE®*** (c.1993) was the sixth in the Bob Mackie series. The replica of the original sketch includes the mask. This jewel multi-color beaded gown accentuates the Mackie perfume bottle.

295. An informative booklet introducing designer Francois Lesage came with the bisque porcelain ***Royal Splendor® BARBIE®*** (1993). Lesage created lavish embroidered designs for the greatest names in haute couture. This spectacular purple satin design has 62,000 hand embroidered stitches. Hard to find.

296. ***City Style™ BARBIE®*** (1993) is from the Classique Collection and one of two dolls designed by Mattel's Janet Goldblatt. The lid of this shown box was personally signed by the designer.

297. ***Opening Night BARBIE®*** (1993) is also from the Classique Collection and the second doll designed by Janet Goldblatt. The raven hair doll wears a beautiful silver and fuchsia two-piece gown. The lid of this shown box was personally signed and dated by the designer.

298. 1993 was the last year of individually sold Classique Collection fashions. These fashions had copies of the original sketches by Mattel designer Janet Goldblatt on the boxes. The two fashions were ***BARBIE® Flower Shower™*** and ***BARBIE® Satin Dreams™***. Both are hard to find. These boxes were personally signed and dated by the designer.

299. ***BARBIE® Flower Shower™*** fashions (1993).

300. BARBIE® Satin Dreams™ fashion (1993).

301. Queen of Hearts™ BARBIE® (1994) was seventh in the Bob Mackie series. The replica of the original sketch shows the turned-up cape collar forming a heart and the heart shaped headdress with feathers. This replica sketch and cape lining was personally signed in silver ink by Bob Mackie, although the majority were not.

302. ***Savy Shopper™ BARBIE®*** (1994) was designed by Nicole Miller. The print on BARBIE® doll's jacket is the designer's signature style. This doll was a Bloomingdale's exclusive.

303. Evening Extravaganza BARBIE® was the Classique Collection's third year edition (1994). The doll was designed by Kitty Black Perkins.

304. ***Goddess Of The Sun® BARBIE®*** (c.1995) was eighth in the Bob Mackie series. The replica of the original sketch has the sun-rays bouncing off the shoulders, as does the doll.

305. ***Donna Karan New York BARBIE®*** was a Bloomingdale's exclusive (1995). This doll was available in blonde or brunette. DKNY is a trademark of Donna Karan.

306. ***Moon Goddess® BARBIE®*** (1996) is the ninth and last doll in this Bob Mackie series. The elaborate replica of the original sketch includes the moon which is wrapped in iridescent sequins.

307. ***Calvin Klein Jeans BARBIE®*** (1996) was initially a Bloomingdale exclusive. The fashion was designed by Calvin Klein. The logo was used with permission.

308. ***City Shopper BARBIE®*** (1996) was a Macy's exclusive designed by Nicole Miller. The coat's lining is a finely detailed print, the designer's signature style. This print is also used on the box graphic. BARBIE® doll's hair color and style resembles Nicole Miller's own.

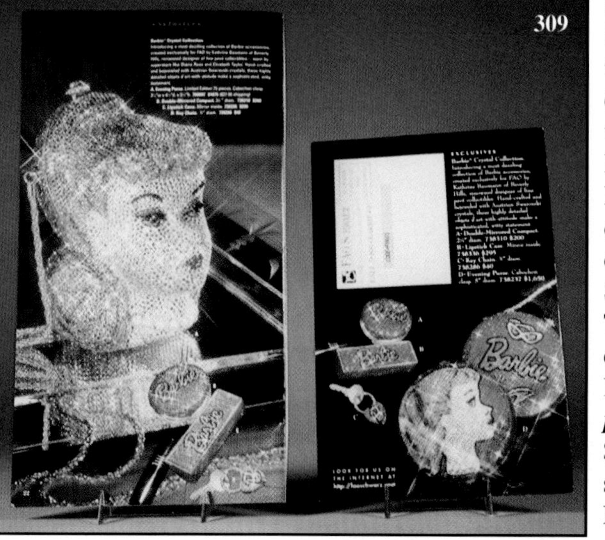

309. This F.A.O. Schwarz exclusive, the ***BARBIE® Crystal Collection*** (1996), was designed by Katherine Bauman of Beverly Hills. Each design was handcrafted of Austrian Swarovski crystals. There were two evening purses — the BARBIE® doll ***logo purse*** retailed for $1,650 and the other, shaped like a ponytail BARBIE® doll head, retailed for $1,875. Other available items included: a lipstick case, retailed for $295; double-mirrored compact, retailed for $200; and key chain, retailed for $40.

Chapter 16

Parchment Paraphernalia

The parchment paraphernalia (paper collectibles) consists of various items from greeting cards to calendars to advertisements. These collectibles are sometimes overlooked in collecting; thus making them hard to find after even a short period of time. Each item offers a different dimensional view of the BARBIE® doll collecting world.

310. This 25¢ off on any BARBIE® doll fashion ***coupon*** appeared in the Sunday comic sections of various newspapers across the U.S. There were 56,110,000 coupons distributed on April 13, 1980.

311. ***Who's Who: The Mattel Licensing Directory*** (c. 1981) was not available to the general public.

312. ***Success for All Seasons*** (1982) Mattel catalogue was not available to the general public.

313. ***Mattel Delivers The Answer Book*** (1983) was not available to the general public.

314. ***Mattel Toys 1984*** catalogue was not available to the general public.

315. ***1985 Answer Book***, Mattel, was not available to the general public.

316. Advertisements slated ***Mardi Gras BARBIE®*** (1988) as the "First in a Series of the American Beauties™". Rare.

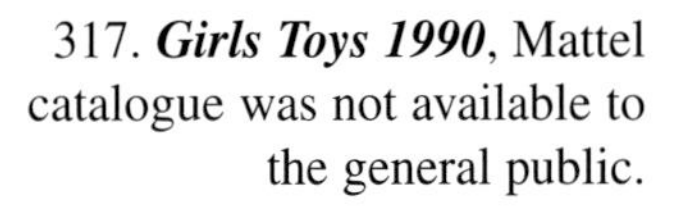

317. ***Girls Toys 1990***, Mattel catalogue was not available to the general public.

318. In 1990, the BARBIE® doll Collectors Club, Great Lakes Chapter of Michigan held a "BARBIE® Grants A Wish" event with proceeds donated to the Make A Wish Foundation. A Mattel representative donated a group of prototype pictures that were auctioned at this event. Shown are five prototype pictures from the group. Theses prototypes were used for illustrative materials in the 1990 Mattel Girls Toys catalogue and fashion booklet.

320. ***BARBIE® For Girls Decorative Border*** (c. 1993-94) was manufactured under license by Borden Home Wall Covering. Perhaps this will become as rare as the Beatles wall covering!!

319. BARBIE® doll had three basic head molds between 1959 to 1989. The first had molded lashes and was used from 1959 to 1966. The second had an updated look and was issued in 1967. The third, known for her smile, is fondly referred to as the SuperStar head after the SuperStar™ BARBIE® doll. A variety of BARBIE® dolls reflecting changing roles and fashions were featured on the fold-out cover of the *Smithsonian* magazine, December 1989.

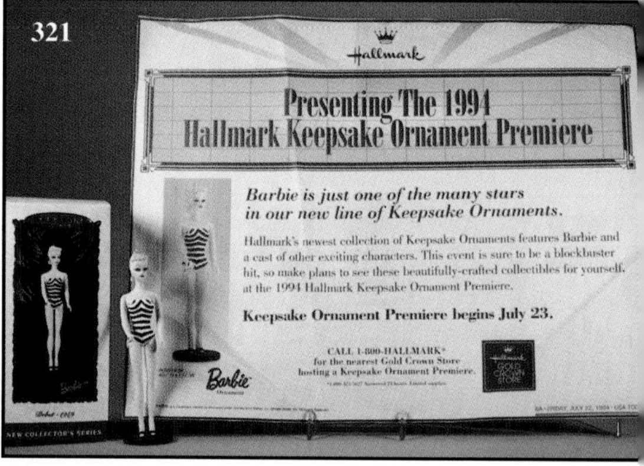

321. This Hallmark Cards advertisement for Gold Crown Stores announces the 1994 Hallmark Keepsake Ornament Premiere. It showcases an actual size photograph of the new collector series ***#1 BARBIE® Debut 1959*** ornament.

322. ***Snow Princess BARBIE®*** doll and a Valentine greeting card made under license by Hallmark Cards, Inc.

323. ***Girls Toys — Celebrating 50 Years***, Mattel catalogue (1995) was not available to the general public.

324. This ***BARBIE®*** ***paperweight*** from Waterford was hand-cut of fine lead crystal by the finest crystal artisans in the world. It features art work from *BARBIE® Sings!*. Bloomingdales offered 100,000 of this exclusive by mail. The item was carried in their 1995 and 1996 catalogs. These paperweights did not come with certificates.

325. ***BARBIE® 1996 Calendar*** was manufactured under license from Mattel, Inc. by Hallmark Cards, Inc. This BARBIE® doll cut-out measures 11-1/2 inches, the height of BARBIE® doll. The fashion is *Commuter Set*.

326. ***Repro Art Book, 1996 Toy Fair Edition*** and the ***1996 Mattel Catalog*** were not available to the general public.

327. The Enesco Corporation has produced numerous items under license from Mattel, Inc. Shown is ***BARBIE® 1996 Catalog***.

328. ***BARBIE® 1997 Calendar*** was manufactured under license from Mattel, Inc. by Hallmark Cards, Inc. The front cover features ***Talking BARBIE®*** doll wearing *All That Jazz*.

Chapter 17

Around The World With International BARBIE® Dolls

In 1980, Mattel introduced the BARBIE® Doll International Collection at the New York Toy Fair. Beginning in 1985, the line name changed to BARBIE® Dolls of the World Collection.

Collectors refer to both of these series as The International BARBIE® doll. The dolls wear delightful costumes that authentically represent a country's culture. Enjoy your trip around the world!

329. Shown is the first series, BARBIE® Doll International Collection with my seminar and slide program pamphlet. Information on these dolls was presented at the National BARBIE® Doll Convention, BARBIE® Loves a Fairy Tale".

330. These International BARBIE® dolls made their debut in 1980: ***Parisian BARBIE® from France*** (discontinued in 1984); ***Royal BARBIE® from England*** (discontinued in 1983); and ***Italian BARBIE®*** (discontinued in 1983). The flags each doll holds were made by the author. Parisian BARBIE® doll wore a cancan dress— the cancan is a French dance known for its high kicking. The cancan became popular around 1840 in the music halls of Paris.

331. ***Oriental BARBIE® from (British) Hong Kong*** (1981-1984) wore a gold cheongsam with Chinese ideograph markings on the shoulder. ***Scottish BARBIE®*** (1981-1984) doll's costume consisted of a Balmoral hat, kilt jacket and the MacQueen tartan. The flags were made by the author.

332. ***India BARBIE®*** (1982-1984) wore an authentic three-piece sari. ***Eskimo BARBIE® from the Arctic*** (1982-1984) wears a genuine design parka. India BARBIE® doll carries a flag made by the author.

333. ***Spanish BARBIE®*** (1983-1985) wears a Flamenco dance costume. ***Swedish BARBIE®***(1983-1985) wears a Midsummer's Eve Festival costume. The flags were made by the author.

334. ***Irish BARBIE***® (1984-1987) and ***Swiss BARBIE***® (1984-1987). The flags were made by the author.

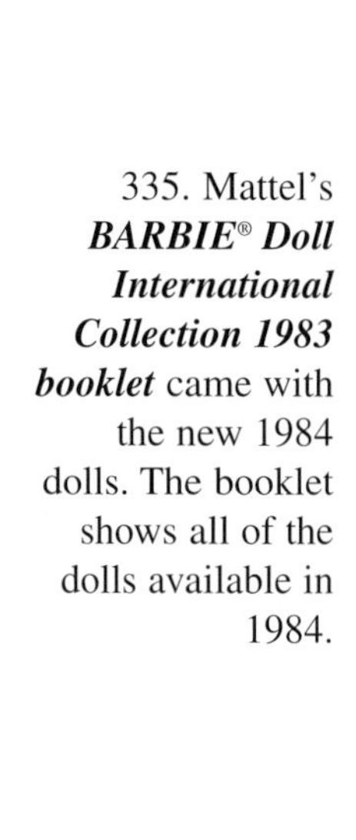

335. Mattel's ***BARBIE® Doll International Collection 1983 booklet*** came with the new 1984 dolls. The booklet shows all of the dolls available in 1984.

336. ***Peruvian BARBIE***® (1986-1988) wears a traditional costume with flowers on the hat. In Peru, women looking for a husband wear flowers on their hats. ***Greek BARBIE***® (1986-1988) wears a Greek Orthodox festival dance costume. The flags were made by the author.

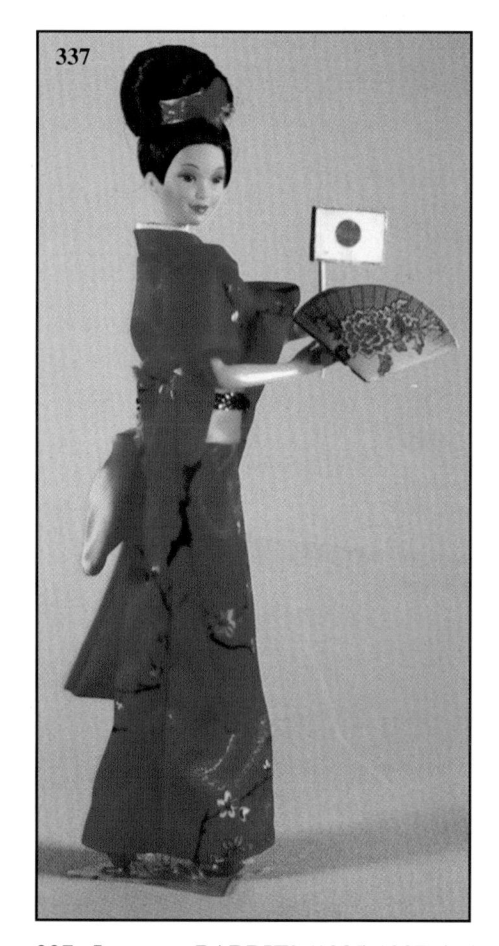

337. ***Japanese BARBIE***® (1985-1987) in her Kimono with obi. This doll was the first doll in the BARBIE® Dolls of the World Collection. The flag was made by the author.

338. ***German BARBIE***® (1987-1988) is dressed in a folk costume worn during Oktoberfest. ***Icelandic BARBIE***® (1987-1988). The flags were made by the author.

339. ***Canadian BARBIE***® (1988-1989) is costumed as a member of the Royal Canadian Mounties. ***Korean BARBIE***® (1988-1989). The flags were made by the author.

340. ***Russian BARBIE***® (1989-1990). ***Mexican BARBIE***® (1989-1990) wore a mock embroidered peasant blouse and orange satin skirt. The flags were made by the author.

341. ***Nigerian BARBIE***® (1990-1991) wears a traditional hot weather dress. ***Brazilian BARBIE® of Rio De Janeiro*** (1990-1991) wears a Samba School dance costume for the annual Carnival Celebration parade. The flags were made by the author.

342. ***Malaysian BARBIE***® (1990-1991) wears the traditional Batik Songket. ***Czechoslovakian BARBIE***® (late 1990-1991) is dressed in the traditional Slovak Festival Costume. The flags were made by the author.

343. ***Russian BARBIE***® (1997). This doll represents a member of the Russian Commonwealth of Independent States. This is not a second edition because the 1989 Russian BARBIE® doll represented Russia as part of the Soviet Union.

344. ***Australian BARBIE***® (1993-1994) wears a typical outfit of an outback jillaroo. The flag was made by the author.

345. ***Jamaican BARBIE***® (1992). The flag made by the author.

346. ***Dutch BARBIE***® (1994-1995) wears the costume of the Volendam, Netherlands people. ***Chinese BARBIE***® (1994-1995) wears a traditional gauzi costume. ***Kenyan BARBIE***® (1994-1995) wears the shuka with a kanga costume. The flags were made by the author.

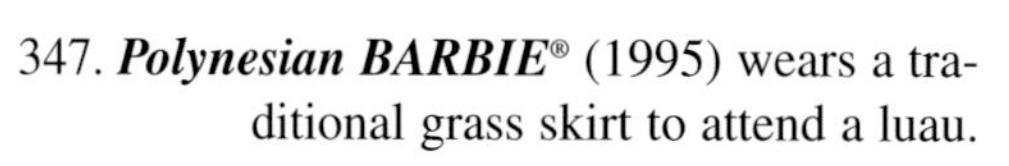

347. ***Polynesian BARBIE***® (1995) wears a traditional grass skirt to attend a luau.

349. ***Norwegian BARBIE***® (1996) is dressed for The National Day — May 17th in Bunad. ***Ghanian BARBIE***® (1996-1997) doll's costume represents the hand-woven cloth called Kentre. The flags were made by the author.

348. ***German BARBIE***® (1995) was not a second edition. This doll represents the reunification of the West and East Germanys. German BARBIE® doll has painted white legs and molded on shoes.

350. ***Puerto Rican BARBIE***® (1997) wears a white dress to attend a festival or party. The flag was made by the author.

352. These ***stickers*** depict various BARBIE® Dolls of the World. They were produced under license by Ambassador-Hallmark Cards, Inc. (c.1996) and were distributed in the U.S. and Canada.

351. ***Russian BARBIE***® (1997) wears a festival costume.

353. ***Native American BARBIE®*** dolls. The first edition was in 1993, second in 1994, third in 1995 and fourth in 1997, a Toys R Us exclusive. Each doll represents a proud Indian heritage, culture and tradition in authentic Native American costumes.

354. McDonald's Restaurants used BARBIE® Dolls of the World dolls as the Happy Meal prize for July 1996. A different figurine was offered each week. The figurines included: ***Dutch BARBIE® figurine, Kenyan BARBIE® figurine, Japanese BARBIE® figurine, Mexican BARBIE® figurine,*** and ***U.S. BARBIE® figurine***. Two box versions were available. These boxes became a BARBIE® doll world. Issued in the U.S. only.

355. The Danbury Mint produced two plates under license, each copyrighted 1992. They were called ***BARBIE® Visits Russia*** and ***BARBIE® Visits England***.

356. ***Native American BARBIE®*** doll joined the Dolls of the World Collection in 1993. Hallmark Cards, Inc., under license from Mattel, introduced a new series of Keepsake Ornaments — Dolls of the World Collection with ***Native American BARBIE®*** in 1996.

357. There have been several variations in International costumes. For example: the fabric on these two Italian BARBIE® dolls are different. The one on the left skirt has no pattern while the one on the right has a vertical pattern. The unusual head mold of Italian BARBIE® doll slightly resembles the SuperStar head mold with the smile but this one has a long, slender nose.

Chapter 18

Happy Holidays Series

The first Happy Holidays BARBIE® doll debuted in November 1988 for an average retail price of $27.00. This first issue was available and marked clearance in some retail stores through January 1989. Although advertising circulars had touted the release of a special holiday season collector doll, the frantic frenzy of recent years was not present.

Enjoy this treasury of Happy Holidays dolls from 1988 through 1996.

358. The first ***Happy Holidays BARBIE***® (1988) wore a holly berry red with silver trim gown. This doll was advertised in several publications and appeared on the cover of *BARBIE® The Magazine For Girls* dated Winter 1989.

359. An advertisement for the ***1989 Happy Holidays BARBIE***® doll with snow flake white was the same photo-art that appeared on the Winter 1990 *BARBIE® The Magazine For Girls.*

360. The Winter 1991 *BARBIE® The Magazine For Girls* cover illustrated the fiery magenta ***Happy Holidays BARBIE***® (1990). This was the first year that the series had both white and black dolls.

361. The Winter 1992 *BARBIE® The Magazine For Girls* cover illustrated the spruce green velvet ***Happy Holidays BARBIE®*** (1991).

362. The ***Mattel, Inc. Report to Shareholders-Third Quarter 1991*** featured the 1991 ***Happy Holiday BARBIE®***.

363. The Holiday 1992 *BARBIE® The Magazine for Girls* cover illustrated the silver ***Happy Holidays BARBIE®*** (1992).

364

364. Holiday BARBIE® Collection — ***3 Display Greeting Cards*** (c. 1995). All were made under license by Hallmark Cards, Inc. Hard to find.

365. The November/December 1993 *BARBIE® The Magazine For Girls* featured the poinsettia red with gold trim, ***Happy Holidays BARBIE®*** (1993) on the cover. The magazine mentions the ***Hallmark Keepsake Ornament - Holiday BARBIE® #1***, shown with Hallmark Shoppe display.

366. The November/December 1994 *BARBIE® The Magazine For Girls* featured the gold ***Happy Holidays BARBIE®*** (1994) on the cover. This was the second year for the ***Hallmark Keepsake Ornament- Holiday BARBIE®***, shown with Hallmark Shoppe display.

367. ***Happy Holiday Collector Print*** features the 1995 Happy Holidays BARBIE® doll; facsimiles signatures of Jill E. Barad, Chief Operating Officer Mattel, Inc. and Kitty Black Perkins, Designer of the 1995 Happy Holidays doll. This print was available by mail from Mattel. Hard to find.

368. ***Happy Holidays BARBIE®*** (1995). The ***Hallmark Keepsake Ornament— Holiday BARBIE® #3*** (1995) was made under license. A McDonald's ***Happy Meal Holiday BARBIE® Figurine*** (1995). Hard to find.

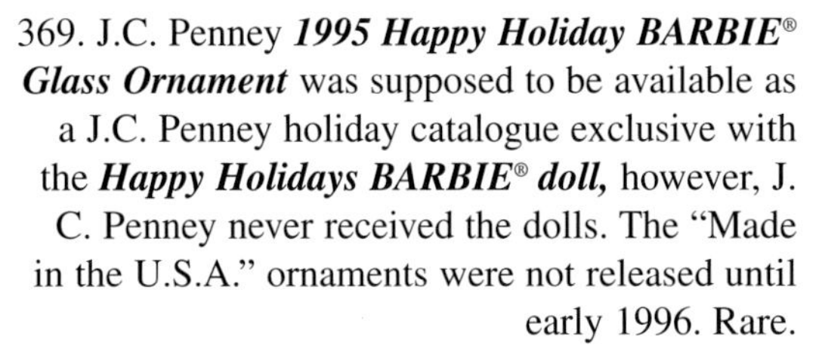
369. J.C. Penney ***1995 Happy Holiday BARBIE® Glass Ornament*** was supposed to be available as a J.C. Penney holiday catalogue exclusive with the ***Happy Holidays BARBIE® doll,*** however, J. C. Penney never received the dolls. The "Made in the U.S.A." ornaments were not released until early 1996. Rare.

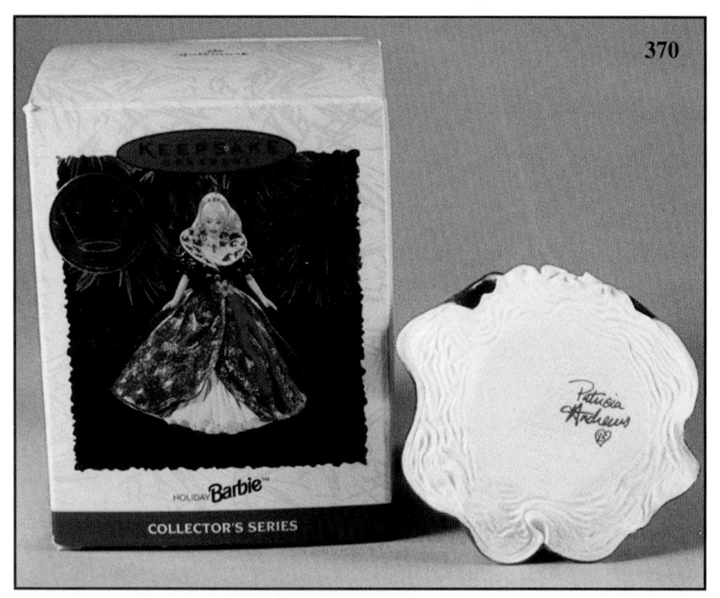

370. This ***Hallmark Keepsake Ornament—Holiday BARBIE® (1995)*** was signed by ornament designer, Patricia Andrews. It was available in very limited quantities at very selected Hallmark Gold-Crown Stores.

371. The Hallmark Keepsake Ornament Collector's Club offered members exclusive 1996 Club Edition ornaments, one of which was based on the 1988 Happy Holidays BARBIE® doll. Also illustrated, the Hallmark Shoppe's promotional for this ornament and the author's membership card.

372. The ***1996 Happy Holidays BARBIE®***; the ***1996 Hallmark Keepsake Ornament—Holiday BARBIE® #4*** with the Hallmark Cards, Inc. store display; and the ***1996 Hallmark Holiday BARBIE® Coloring and Activity book***. This book was produced under license by Golden Books Publishing Company, Inc. It was free with any three Hallmark greeting cards purchased.

373. ***Happy Holidays BARBIE®*** doll (1996) with a ***Happy Holidays BARBIE® doll decoupage ornament*** (1996) made under license by Matrix Industries, Ltd.

Chapter 19

MISCELLANEOUS THING-AM-A-JIGS

The items illustrated and described within this chapter are diverse, thus, "miscellaneous thing-am-a-jigs".

374. ***Deluxe Reading Dream Kitchen*** (1963-1964). Very hard to find. This item was sold through the Montgomery Wards catalogue, although today it is mostly sold by the individual piece. The dishwasher worked with water, as did the sink. The range had light-up burners and the oven had a turning rotisserie which required two "C" batteries.

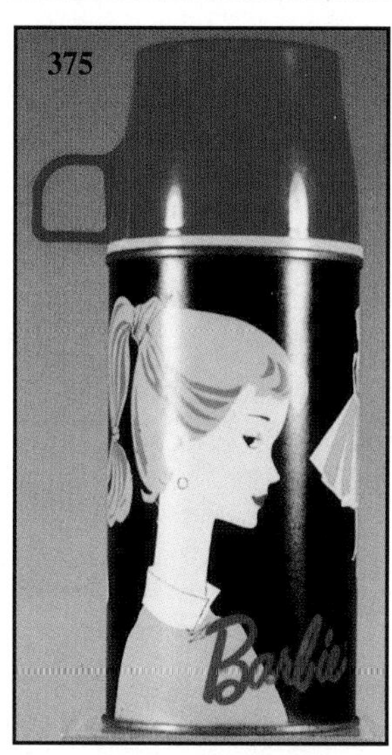

375. ***BARBIE® Thermos® Bottle No. 2025H*** (c. 1962) from Canada, although some were available in various regions in the U.S. It features a ponytail BARBIE® doll and #900 Series fashions in color variations of the actual fashions. This is the very first BARBIE® Thermos Bottle and is hard to find.

376. This pewter dinner set has a fun daisy motif. The table is from ***BARBIE® 'N Skipper Go Together Furniture, Dining Room Furniture*** (1965). Hard to find.

378. The ***World of BARBIE® Thermos® Lunch Box*** (c.1971) is a 'mod' era lunch box with colorful illustrations of never produced fashions. (Thermos Division — King Seeley Thermos Co.).

377. These 45 RPM records came with Live Action BARBIE® doll on stage entitled ***I'm Happy I'm BARBIE®***; 'Live Action Ken® doll on stage entitled ***A Little Bit of That Sky***; and 'Live Action P. J. doll on stage entitled ***Hey Little P. J. Gal***. Each record had a vocal and an instrumental of its song title. For more BARBIE® tunes see Chapter 7, Groovy Vibrations and Melodies in *Treasury of BARBIE® Doll Accessories*.

379. To those of you who inquired, "What is the dress-form in illustration 222 of *Treasury of BARBIE® Doll Accessories*? Answer: The white ***BARBIE® dress-form*** is from the Mattel Sew Magic™ Machine BARBIE® Fashion Set (c. 1973).

380. ***BARBIE® Portable Phonograph*** was a line of cast-iron items produced by Durham Industries Inc. (c.1976). Rare.

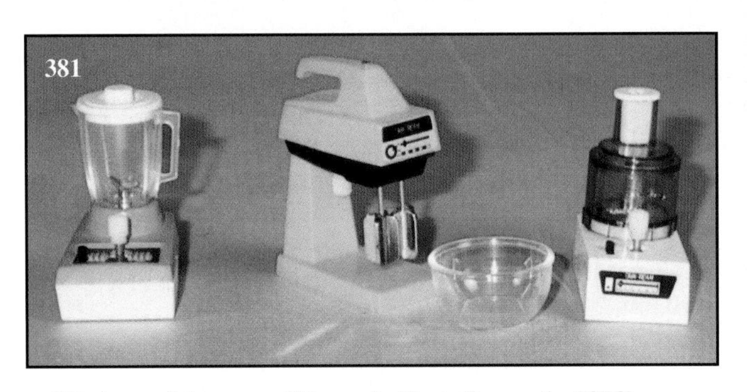

381 A set of three ***small household appliances*** (c. 1978) were available from the Sears Roebuck and Company catalogue.

382. Takara photo-art ***paper dolls*** (undated). Takara produced BARBIE® and Ken® dolls in the mid-80s for Japanese distribution.

383. ***BARBIE® Finishing Touches — Pretty Closets™*** (c. 1985). BARBIE® doll needs a shoe/purse bag to organize coordinating shoes and purses for fashion ensembles. Hard to find

NEW

I'M INTO BARBIE™
Brush And Comb Her gorgeous face graces a full brush of durable plastic bristles; coordinating plastic comb is heart-shaped. Brush, 6¼" long. Comb, 3¾" wide. Packaged in gift carton. Ages 3 and up.
Reg. $12.00
SPECIAL $9.99 the set

I'M INTO BARBIE™
Cologne Light, exclusively Barbie. 1.9 fl. oz. Reg. $6.00
SPECIAL $4.99

BARBIE and I'M INTO BARBIE are trademarks owned by and used under license from Mattel, Inc.
© Mattel, Inc. 1989. All rights reserved.

100

NEW
I'M INTO BARBIE™ Gift Set
If she's into bubbly baths and soft-scented dusting powder, this is the gift for her. 4 fl. oz. of bubble bath and 2 oz. net wt. of dusting powder come in a matching Barbie gift carton.
Ages 3 and up. Reg. $8.00
SPECIAL $5.99 the set

FOR A VERY Barbie CHRISTMAS!

I'M INTO BARBIE™ Collection
For girls ages 3 to 10.
A. Earrings Pierced only, with surgical steel posts. ¾" long. Plastic. Reg. $5.00 $3.99
B. Necklace Center heart with Barbie on one side, place for photo on the other. 14½" long. Plastic. Reg. $9.00 $6.99
C. Bracelet Plastic with heart and pearlized beads. Sizes 5½" or 6½". Reg. $6.00 $4.99
SPECIALS

101

384. Avon in their 1989 Holiday catalogue had a line called "I'm into BARBIE®"; it was produced under license. This line consisted of a ***brush & comb; cologne; bubble bath & dusting powder; pierced earrings; necklace and bracelet.***

385. ***BARBIE® Pretty Treasures*** (c.1995) were very high-quality realistic items produced by Mattel, Inc. These items could be hard to find as they did not remain on the toy shelves for long.

386. BARBIE® So Much To Do!™ sets (c. 1995) include: ***Gardenin' Pretty, Cleanin' House, Makin' Breakfast*** and ***Country Fair Fun***.

387. ***Nostalgic BARBIE® Charm Pin*** (1995) was available in sterling silver (as shown) and 14-Karat gold over sterling silver. Under license and designed by Michael Anthony Jewelers, Inc.

388. ***BARBIE® Long-Distance Greetings*** (c.1995) was made under license from Mattel, Inc. by Hallmark Cards, Inc. This item includes a Sprint prepaid long-distance phone card. It was not widely distributed. Perhaps it was for the Kansas City area, where the corporate headquarters of both Hallmark and Sprint are located. Rare.

389. A variety of ***BARBIE® Single Use Flash Camera & Film All in One*** (c. 1995) made under license by Kalimar, Inc. The three shown designs are: ***Baywatch™ BARBIE®***, ***BARBIE®*** and ***Hot Skatin BARBIE®***.

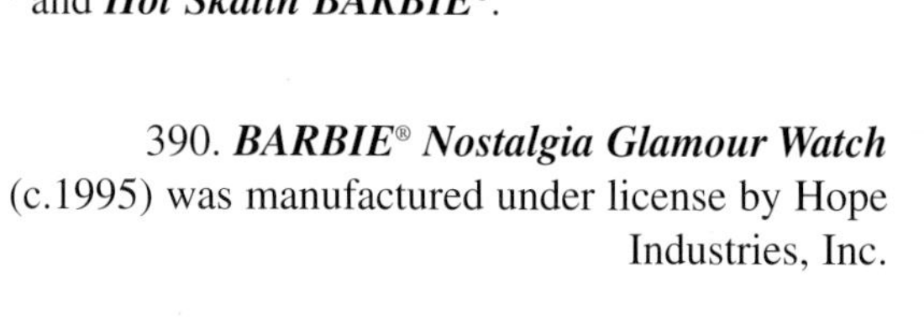

390. ***BARBIE® Nostalgia Glamour Watch*** (c.1995) was manufactured under license by Hope Industries, Inc.

391. This keychain series (1996) was produced under license from Mattel by Basic Fun Inc. ***Original BARBIE***® and ***Solo In the Spotlight BARBIE***® were a Q. V. C. (cable shopping channel) exclusive set. ***Original BARBIE***®, ***Solo In the Spotlight BARBIE***®, ***Picnic Set BARBIE***®, ***Poodle Parade BARBIE***® and ***BARBIE***® ***& Ken***® ***Set*** were available in various retail locations.

392. Russell Stover Candies — ***BARBIE***® ***- Chocolate Eggs*** (1997). Four different designs of this item came in egg-shaped tins. Note: Remove the chocolate before saving this item.

393. ***Classic BARBIE***® ***Ornaments*** (1996) were a series of twelve ornaments produced under license and sold exclusively by Ashton-Drake.

394. Russell Stover Candies — ***BARBIE***® ***Solid Milk Chocolate Hearts*** (c.1996). These valentine heart shaped tins came with various BARBIE® doll photo-art. Note: Remove the chocolate before saving this item.

395. The 30th anniversary of Star Trek was celebrated in 1996 with a special ***BARBIE***® ***and Ken***® ***Star Trek***™ ***Gift Set*** and a ***Star Trek***™ ***BARBIE***® ***and Ken***® ***Collector Timepiece*** (manufactured by Hope Industries, Inc. under license from Mattel, Inc.)

Chapter 20

A How to Guide on Scene Composition and Tips

Add zing to your BARBIE® collection by creating scenes of like dolls, fashion and accessories. You may have the same collectibles as your friend but with a scene, no two people will create exactly the same set. Have fun and be creative.

Tips for successful scene presentations:

1. Enjoy what you collect.
2. Collect coordinating themes of dolls, accessories and fashions.
3. Dolls should have fashions and accessories of their time period. Some time periods overlap. It is acceptable to group dolls together if a vast time difference does not exist.
4. Be creative. Purchase items at craft and hobby stores to add extra special touches.
5. See the four guide steps to creating a successful scene presentation.

Remember, no two scenes will ever look the same. Be unique in your design.

396. Be creative and capture the emotion of a special moment. Here BARBIE® and Ken® dolls share their special day with friends. Use as many or as little detail as you desire.

Step 1

397. Shop around for coordinating accessories. Here I have chosen Mattel's ***Nibbles™ Horse*** and the ***BARBIE® Feeding Fun Stable™ Playset***. Nibbles is illustrated on the box of the Fun Stable Playset. The two pair together perfectly.

Step 2

398. Familiarize yourself with the various parts then read the instructions before assembling. Take care not to break any pieces.

Step 3

399. After assembling the playset, accumulate other related items if any were produced. Decide how to best display the scene. Remember to plan your available space accordingly. Then add dolls in appropriate ensembles to then theme and time period.

Step 4

400. Here is a finished scene composition featuring ***Nibbles*** and the ***Feeding Fun Stable***. The added straw bundles were purchased at a craft store. What an added touch!

Ten Most Frequently Asked Collecting Questions

1. Is there a way to determine the date of an item by its logo?

Yes. Mattel has had several BARBIE® logos throughout the years. See illustrations 401 — 406 and the corresponding captions for definitive years of use.

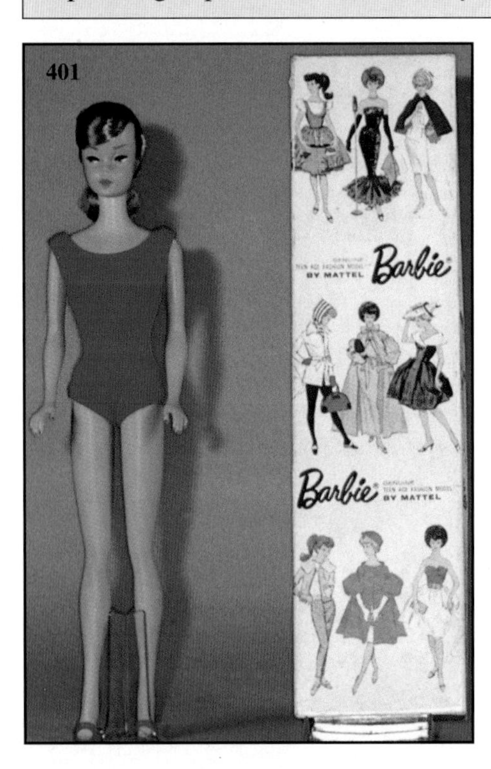

401. The first trademark was a signature with a sharp, upward stroked "e". This logo was used from 1959 to 1969. It is shown on the box of a 1964 Swirl Ponytail BARBIE® doll.

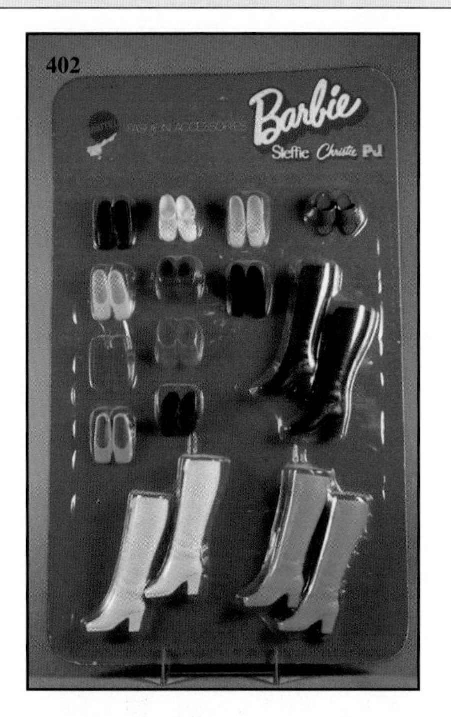

402. The second logo featured a shadow effect around the first signature trademark and appeared on packages from 1970 to 1975. As illustrated on a package of ***BARBIE® Fashion Accessories Shoes*** (c. 1971).

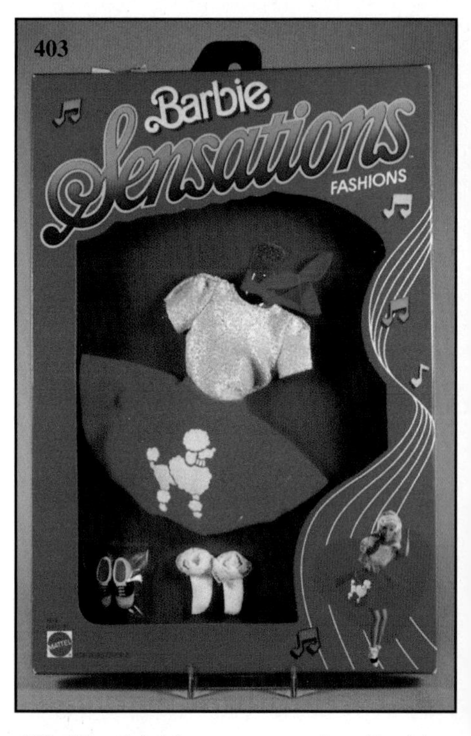

403. The third logo was a printed/writing style with a fancy capital "B" with shadow effect. It was used from 1976 to 1990. This logo is illustrated on ***BARBIE® and The Sensations™ Fashions — #4978, Poodle Skirt*** (1988).

2. Are there different eras of BARBIE® dolls, accessories and fashions as there are in antiques and collectibles?

Yes. There is an age of dollectibility (doll collectibles) which is accepted by experienced collectors.

The Golden Years or ***Vintage*** (1959-1972). Ruth Handler, the creator of BARBIE® doll, oversaw the line through these years.

Classic (1973-1988)

Contemporary (1989 to present)

3. Were all vintage items made in Japan?

No. Not all vintage items were made in Japan. While the majority of dolls and fashions were imported from Japan, some dolls may have been made in the U.S. Many accessories were manufactured within the U.S. For example: the SPP (Standard Plastic Products) cases and trunks were made in New Jersey; Suzy Goose toys were made in Michigan; and paperboard accessories were made in Illinois. The bits and pieces of fashion ensembles were manufactured by dollhouse miniature companies in the U.S.

Throughout the years BARBIE® doll merchandise has been produced and distributed to and from various global locations.

4. Is the date imprinted on the doll or accessory an accurate date of issue?

The imprinted date is the copyright date of the item. For example: Dolls imprinted with "1966" continue to be produced 30 plus years since that time. Also, copyright dates on packages and booklets are sometimes a year before its date of issue.

5. Are the items made today as collectible as things made in the past?

Yes, the "Contemporary" period has innumerable unique lines with items having great potential dollectibility. Even items which seem to be mass produced today could possibly be rare and hard to find tomorrow.

6. What BARBIE® doll and accessory category is the best investment?

There is no guarantee of an investment potential on items of collectibility as values fluctuate. Collect what you like for collecting's sake not as a potential investment.

7. What is the best way to collect accessories? In the box or displayed?

404. The fourth logo has been used since 1989 through 1997 on nostalgic collectibles and various special editions. It is similar to the first trademark yet the difference is in the shortness of the ending stroke of the "e". Illustrated on the box and watch-face of the Fossil Watch, ***Solo In The Spotlight,*** sterling silver (1994).

The accessories are worth more in NRFB (Never Removed From Box) or MIB (Mint in Box) condition. Since the majority of accessories do require assembly and take-up more space, it is up to the individual collector. Personally, I prefer to display the items as scenes.

8. What is the difference if any, between limited edition and special edition?

A limited edition states its specific edition and often comes with certificate. Whereas a special edition is produced as a store exclusive or for a special occasion.

9. Do items that state "collectible" have the potential to be collectible?

Yes, there are many unique items which are specifically made for collectors. As with anything, collect what you enjoy and enjoy what you collect.

10. Is the first in a series always the most valuable?

Not necessarily. It depends on the secondary market supply and demand. If there are scant quantities of an item and the people who desire that particular item out-number the quantity, then the market reflects this.

405. The fifth logo was a printed-writing style. It was used on items beginning in the middle of 1990 and continues to be used through 1997 . Illustrated on ***Golden Paper Doll Book BARBIE® #1502-5*** (c. 1993).

406. The sixth logo was the same printed style with a shadow effect beginning in 1995 through 1997. Illustrated on ***BARBIE® and the Scavenger Hunt***, c.1996 — A Little Golden Book.

EPILOGUE

This second book has been written by popular demand, to enable the collector in pursuing their collecting quest.

Collecting is an adventure — around the corner may be what has been searched for, for years. It might be something you just saw in the toy isle.

The endeavor of this book was to expand the horizons of the collector to the multi-dimensional world of BARBIE® doll, accessories and fashions collecting.

THE BARBIE® FAMILY TREE

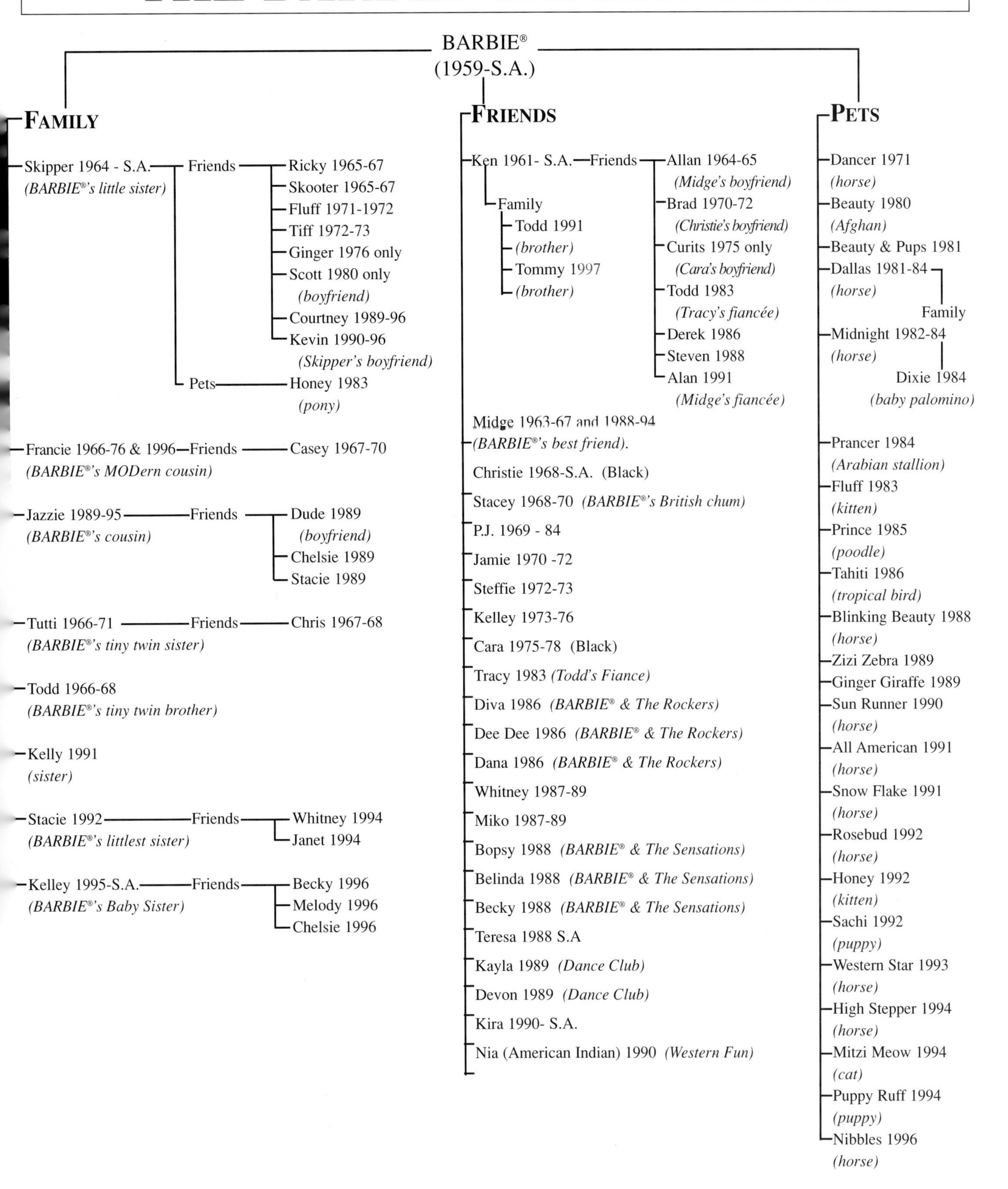

S.A. = Still available in the United States

PRICE GUIDE

Illus. #	Item	Price	I Want	I Have
	INTRODUCTION			
	Enchanted Seasons Collection™			
1	Snow Princess™	$140	❑	❑
1	Spring Bouquet®	130	❑	❑
1	Autumn Glory™	125	❑	❑
1	Summer Splendor™	85	❑	❑
	CHAPTER 1 — HISTORY OF BARBIE® DOLL COLLECTING			
3	Signed Ruth Handler Photograph	$300	❑	❑
4	The World of BARBIE® — The			
	BARBIE® Magazine Annual (1964)	75	❑	❑
	Skipper fashion — Me 'N My Doll	225	❑	❑
	Tutti fashion — Let's Play BARBIE® doll	275	❑	❑
6	Montgomery Wards' Original BARBIE® doll	775	❑	❑
7	The International BARBIE® Doll Collectors Club Gazette	5 each	❑	❑
8	BARBIE® Loves New York,1984 convention souvenir book	25	❑	❑
9	Sears Celebration™ Barbie doll	100	❑	❑
10	"Vive Les Bebes" Fashionably BARBIE® Luncheon Centerpiece	175	❑	❑
11	Blue Rhapsody™	850	❑	❑
12	Enchanted Evening™	500	❑	❑
13	Benefit Performance™	550	❑	❑
	Benefit Performance™ doll advertisement	12	❑	❑
14	Wedding Party™	675	❑	❑
15	Solo in the Spotlight™	235	❑	❑
16	Sophisticated Lady™	255	❑	❑
17	Dance Magic™ BARBIE™ Grants A Wish	75	❑	❑
18	BARBIE™ Loves A Fairy Tale Convention dolls	550	❑	❑
19	The Magic of BARBIE® in Birmingham memorabilia	750	❑	❑
20	Print by Artist Catena Lemonakis	45	❑	❑
21	50th Golden Anniversary BARBIE® doll			
	United States distribution	495	❑	❑
	Global distribution	375	❑	❑
22-23	BARBIE® and the Bandstand convention package including Bandstand Beauty BARBIE® doll	1150	❑	❑
24	BARBIE® and the Bandstand Carrying Case	85	❑	❑
25	"BARBIE™ Sings 60's Style" compact disc	35	❑	❑
26-27	Leader of the Pack Luncheon Centerpiece	250	❑	❑
28	Dancin' Party™	225	❑	❑
	CHAPTER 2 — BIRTHDAYS AND ANNIVERSARIES			
30	BARBIE®'s Sweet 16	$60	❑	❑
31	Kissing BARBIE®	50	❑	❑
32	"BARBIE® Turns 21", *Life Magazine* article	25	❑	❑
33	Crystal BARBIE®	35	❑	❑
	Crystal Ken®	35	❑	❑
34	BARBIE® Silver 'Vette	85	❑	❑
36	Collector Series III — Silver Sensation fashion	40	❑	❑
37	Blue Rhapsody™	850	❑	❑
	Blue Rhapsody™ doll advertisement	18	❑	❑
38	SuperStar BARBIE®	30	❑	❑
	SuperStar Ken®	30	❑	❑
39	Wedding Party™	675	❑	❑
	Wedding Party™ doll advertisement	30	❑	❑
40	F.A.O. Schwarz- Golden Greetings™	350	❑	❑
	F.A.O. Schwarz -Golden Greetings™ doll advertisement	15	❑	❑
41	35th Anniversary BARBIE® (Brunette)	60	❑	❑
	BARBIE® Brunette Debut	35	❑	❑
42	35th Anniversary BARBIE® (Blonde)	45	❑	❑
	35th Anniversary BARBIE® Blonde Gift Set	175	❑	❑
43	35th Anniversary Festival BARBIE®	600	❑	❑
44	30th Anniversary 1961 Ken®	250	❑	❑
45	30th Anniversary 1964 Skipper	140	❑	❑
	CHAPTER 3 — THE RAREST ARCHITECTURE			
	Note: The prices quoted are for mint and complete structures.			
46	BARBIE® and Ken® Little Theater	$530	❑	❑
	Little Theater Costumes: — "Guinevere"	200	❑	❑
	"King Arthur"	200	❑	❑
47-51	BARBIE® and Skipper School	590	❑	❑
	Skipper fashion, School Girl	185	❑	❑
512-55	Skipper Dream Room	375	❑	❑
	Skipper doll with Lifelike Bendable Legs	155	❑	❑
	Skipper fashion, Rainy Day Checkers	220	❑	❑
53	Skipper fashion, Dreamtime	60	❑	❑
	Skipper fashion pak, Wooly P.J.'s	25	❑	❑
	Skooter doll	165	❑	❑
56-61	BARBIE® Goes To College — Campus	545	❑	❑
	BARBIE® fashion, Cheerleader	135	❑	❑
	Ken® fashion, Campus Hero	110	❑	❑
61	BARBIE®'s Sports Car	250	❑	❑
	BARBIE® and Ken® Hot Rod	285	❑	❑
62	BARBIE® Café Today	235	❑	❑
	Twist 'N Turn doll	185	❑	❑
	BARBIE® fashion, Ruffles 'N Swirls	60	❑	❑
63	Live Action BARBIE®	145	❑	❑
	Live Action Ken®	100	❑	❑

	Live Action P.J.	125	❑	❑
	CHAPTER 4 — LEISURE TIME FUN			
64	BARBIE® and Ken Hot Rod	$285	❑	❑
65	BARBIE® Country Camper™	70	❑	❑
	Dramatic New Living BARBIE® doll	175	❑	❑
	New Living Skipper doll	65	❑	❑
	Talking Ken® fashion, Shore Lines	115	❑	❑
66	BARBIE® Pool Party		❑	❑
	1st Issue, 1973	60	❑	❑
	2nd Issue, 1974	45	❑	❑
68	BARBIE® Sunsailer™	115	❑	❑
69	BARBIE® Dream Boat™	150	❑	❑
70	BARBIE® Bubbling Spa	45	❑	❑
	Sun Gold—Malibu® BARBIE® doll	25	❑	❑
	Sun Gold—Malibu® Ken® doll	25	❑	❑
	Sun Gold—Malibu® Skipper doll	30	❑	❑
	Sun Gold—Malibu® P. J. doll	35	❑	❑
71	BARBIE® Motor Bike	40	❑	❑
72	Toys R Us BARBIE® & Ken Tennis Stars™ Gift Set	85	❑	❑
	Tennis BARBIE® doll	45	❑	❑
	Tennis Ken® doll	40	❑	❑
	Tennis Skipper doll	35	❑	❑
73	Ken® So Much to Do!		❑	❑
	Weight Liftin' Fun	10	❑	❑
	Surfin' Action	10	❑	❑
75	BARBIE® Mini Van (retail)	30	❑	❑
	CHAPTER 5 — THE IMAGE OF EQUINE			
76	Dancer™	$75	❑	❑
77	BARBIE® Fox Hollow Stables	150	❑	❑
78	Dallas™ Golden Palomino Horse	40	❑	❑
	Western BARBIE® doll	35	❑	❑
79	Midnight™ Black Stallion	40	❑	❑
	Western Ken® doll	32	❑	❑
80	Western Fashions		❑	❑
	BARBIE® — Western Elegance!	22	❑	❑
	Ken® — Western Fringe!	22	❑	❑
82	Honey™, Skipper doll's Show Pony	35	❑	❑
	Western Skipper doll	30	❑	❑
83	BARBIE® Designer Collection — Horseback Riding	20	❑	❑
84	Dixie Baby Palomino	30	❑	❑
85	Arabian Stallion Prancer™	55	❑	❑
	Loving You BARBIE® doll	55	❑	❑
86	Western Fun™ BARBIE® doll	30	❑	❑
	Western Fun™ Ken® doll	40	❑	❑
	Western Fun™ Nia Doll	95	❑	❑
	Western Fun™ Horse — Sun Runner™	45	❑	❑
	Western Fun™ Pet Collie—Turquoise™	30	❑	❑
87	BARBIE® Dream Carriage/Sleigh	95	❑	❑
89	Dear BARBIE® Riding Champion (book — retail)	3	❑	❑
90	Western Stampin'™ BARBIE® & Western Star Gift Set	30	❑	❑
91	Nibbles™ (Retail)	22	❑	❑
92	BARBIE® Feeding Fun Stable™ (Retail)	22	❑	❑
94	Sweet Magnolia™ BARBIE® doll (brunette)	35	❑	❑
	Sweet Magnolia™ Horse & Carriage Set	55	❑	❑
	CHAPTER 6 — BARBIE® FASHIONS IN *LIFE MAGAZINE*, AUGUST 23RD, 1963			
	Life Magazine - August 23rd, 1963 issue	$35	❑	❑
	Note: The prices quoted are for mint and complete fashion ensembles.			
95	#954 Career Girl	145	❑	❑
96	#991 Registered Nurse	100	❑	❑
	#982 Solo In the Spotlight	195	❑	❑
97	#965 Nighty Negligee	60	❑	❑
98	#921 Floral Petticoat	30	❑	❑
99	#973 Sweet Dreams (Yellow)	45	❑	❑
100	#943 Fancy Free	30	❑	❑
101	#975 Winter Holiday	80	❑	❑
102	#931 Garden Party	55	❑	❑
103	#988 Singing In The Shower	75	❑	❑
104	#942 Ice Breaker	60	❑	❑
105	#992 Golden Elegance	195	❑	❑
	#961 Evening Splendor	150	❑	❑
106	#940 Mood For Music	90	❑	❑
107	#946 Dinner At Eight	85	❑	❑
108	#958 Party Date	125	❑	❑
109	#951 Senior Prom	145	❑	❑
110	#949 Rain Coat	40	❑	❑
111	#933 Movie Date	45	❑	❑
112	#915 Peachy Fleecy Coat	95	❑	❑
113	#955 Swingin' Easy	90	❑	❑
114	#937 Sorority Meeting	70	❑	❑
115	#941 Tennis Anyone?	85	❑	❑
116	#987 Orange Blossom	65	❑	❑
117	#944 Masquerade	90	❑	❑
118	#959 Theater Date	85	❑	❑
119	#984 American Airlines Stewardess	105	❑	❑
120	#945 Graduation	45	❑	❑
121	#983 Enchanted Evening	175	❑	❑
122	#967 Picnic Set	165	❑	❑

123	#957 Knitting Pretty (Navy Blue)	115	❏	❏
124	#989 Ballerina	65	❏	❏
125	#948 Ski Queen	100	❏	❏
126	#953 BARBIE® Baby-Sits	140	❏	❏
127	#956 Busy Morning	85	❏	❏
128	#934 After Five	70	❏	❏
129	#979 Friday Night Date	110	❏	❏
130	#986 Sheath Sensation	50	❏	❏
131	#993 Sophisticated Lady	190	❏	❏
132	#939 Red Flare	70	❏	❏
133	#947 Brides Dream	145	❏	❏
	CHAPTER 7 — FASHION BOOKLETS 1959 TO 1997			
	BARBIE® Teen-Age Fashion Model — 1959 - 1st edition	$65	❏	❏
	1959 - 2nd edition	50	❏	❏
	1960 - 3rd edition	35	❏	❏
134-136	BARBIE® Teen-Age Fashion Model and Barbie's Boyfriend			
	Ken® He's a Doll — Pink cover	30	❏	❏
	Blue cover	25	❏	❏
137	Pamphlets — The BARBIE® Game — Queen of the Prom	10	❏	❏
	Now BARBIE® Sings!	15	❏	❏
	BARBIE® Dream House	12	❏	❏
138	BARBIE® Teen-Age Fashion Model and BARBIE®'s Boyfriend			
	Ken® He's a doll! and BARBIE®'s Best Friend Midge	20 each	❏	❏
139	Exclusive Fashions by Mattel	15 each	❏	❏
141	New! Skipper — BARBIE®'s Little Sister	12	❏	❏
142	Junior Edition Styles for Skipper, Skooter and Ricky	18	❏	❏
143	Exclusive Fashions by Mattel	12	❏	❏
144	Junior Edition Styles for Skipper, BARBIE®'s Little Sister	15	❏	❏
145	Tutti—BARBIE® and Skipper's Tiny Sister	20	❏	❏
	Francie—BARBIE®'s MOD'ern Cousin	15	❏	❏
	The World of BARBIE® Fashions and Playthings by Mattel	40 each	❏	❏
	The World of BARBIE® Fashions by Mattel — un-numbered	15	❏	❏
	consecutively numbered	15 each	❏	❏
147	The World of BARBIE® Fashions (1967)	12 each	❏	❏
150	BARBIE®'s World: Bright, Swinging, Now	12	❏	❏
151	The World of BARBIE® Fashions (1968)	12 each	❏	❏
152	Living BARBIE® As full of life as you are.	10	❏	❏
153	Living BARBIE® and Living Skipper	10 each	❏	❏
154	The Lively World of BARBIE®	16	❏	❏
155	The Beautiful World of BARBIE® — (1972)	14	❏	❏
	(1973)	14	❏	❏
156	World of BARBIE® Fashions — (1976)	12	❏	❏
157	BARBIE® World of Fashions — (1978)	10	❏	❏
	(1979)	10 each	❏	❏
	(1980)	10	❏	❏
	BARBIE® World of Fashion (1981) — #0007-3130	10	❏	❏
	#0007-3130 G3	8	❏	❏
	BARBIE® World of Fashion (1982) — #0007-4100	10	❏	❏
	#0007-4100 G1	8	❏	❏
	My First BARBIE® (1982)	12	❏	❏
	Barbie World of Fashion (1983 to 1988)	7 each	❏	❏
	My First BARBIE® (1986)	4	❏	❏
	Skipper A Great Year!—Teen Scrapbook	12	❏	❏
	Skipper Teen Sister of BARBIE®	10	❏	❏
	Booklets (1990-1996)	5 each	❏	❏
	CHAPTER 8 — FAMILY AND FRIENDS			
159	Midge doll with side glance eyes and teeth	275	❏	❏
	Allan doll	150	❏	❏
	Ken® fashion, Saturday Date	85	❏	❏
160	Portrait of Skipper (The Story of Skipper—A New Doll)	18	❏	❏
161	Tutti & Todd dolls	250	❏	❏
162	Ricky doll	145	❏	❏
163	Twist ' N Turn Casey doll	270	❏	❏
	Francie fashion, Pazam!	175	❏	❏
164	Twist 'N Turn Stacey doll	250	❏	❏
	BARBIE® fashion, Togetherness	135	❏	❏
165	Francie doll with Growin 'Pretty Hair	275	❏	❏
166	Walk Lively Steffie doll	250	❏	❏
167	Growing Up Skipper doll	75	❏	❏
	Growing Up Ginger doll	75	❏	❏
168	Super Teen Skipper doll	75	❏	❏
	Skipper's boyfriend, Scott doll	85	❏	❏
169	BARBIE® & Friends Gift Set	80	❏	❏
170	Sweet Roses P. J. doll	60	❏	❏
171	Tropical Miko doll	35	❏	❏
	BARBIE® The Magazine for Girls (Summer 1996)	10	❏	❏
172	Tracy, Bride doll	70	❏	❏
	Todd, Groom doll	60	❏	❏
	Tracy & Todd Wedding Play Pak	45	❏	❏
173	Jewel Secrets Whitney doll	80	❏	❏
174	Teen Dance Jazzie doll	35	❏	❏
175	Western Fun Nia doll	95	❏	❏
176	Wedding Party Midge Gift Set	200	❏	❏
177	*BARBIE® The Magazine for Girls* (Summer 1991)	16	❏	❏
178	Wedding Day Kelly & Todd Gift Set	85	❏	❏
179	Wedding Fantasy BARBIE® & Ken® Gift Set	100	❏	❏
180	Phone Fun Skipper doll	12	❏	❏
	Phone Fun Courtney doll	12	❏	❏
	Skipper fashion, #14383	8	❏	❏

	Skipper fashion, #15891	8	❑	❑
181	Winter Holiday BARBIE® Gift Set	40	❑	❑
	Big Brother Ken® and Baby Brother Tammy dolls (Retail)	15	❑	❑
	CHAPTER 9 — KEYS TO FAME...THE CAREERS			
183	BARBIE®'s Keys to Fame Game	$85	❑	❑
184	Ken® fashion, American Airlines Captain	330	❑	❑
	BARBIE® fashion, American Airlines Stewardess	235	❑	❑
185	BARBIE® fashion, Career Girl	290	❑	❑
186	BARBIE® fashion, Solo In the Spotlight	340	❑	❑
187	BARBIE® fashion, Registered Nurse	185	❑	❑
188	BARBIE® The Baby Sitter (book)	25	❑	❑
189	Bendable legs BARBIE® doll with American Girl Hair Style	660	❑	❑
	BARBIE® fashion, #1635 Fashion Editor	285	❑	❑
190	BARBIE® fashion, #7700 Get-Ups 'N Go	65	❑	❑
	Ken® fashion, #7705 Get-Ups 'N Go	65	❑	❑
191	Day-to-Night™ BARBIE® doll	45	❑	❑
	Day-to-Night™ Ken® doll	40	❑	❑
192	Rappin' Rockin' BARBIE® doll	48	❑	❑
194	Astronaut™ BARBIE® doll	85 each	❑	❑
	"The Dolls Dreams Are Made of" advertisement	15	❑	❑
195	BARBIE® Rockin', Rappin', Dancin' World Tour- Pop-up Book	10	❑	❑
196	F.A.O. Schwarz Silver Screen BARBIE® doll	280	❑	❑
197	Teacher BARBIE® doll, Hispanic (Retail)	25	❑	❑
	Teacher BARBIE® Classroom (Retail)	10	❑	❑
198	Busy Gal™ BARBIE® doll	65	❑	❑
	Busy Gal™ advertisement	5	❑	❑
199	Pet Doctor BARBIE® doll (Retail)	20	❑	❑
	Pet Doctor Check-Up and Play Center (Retail)	15	❑	❑
200	BARBIE® So Much To Do!™ Bank	20	❑	❑
	BARBIE® fashion, #14980 Fashion Avenue	10	❑	❑
	Ken® fashion, #13567 Fashion Avenue	10	❑	❑
	Skipper fashion, #14383	8	❑	❑
	CHAPTER 10 — "... AND NOW A WORD FROM OUR SPONSOR"			
201	Angel Face™ BARBIE® doll	$50	❑	❑
	BARBIE® The Magazine for Girls, Premier Issue (Winter 1984)	20	❑	❑
202	BARBIE® Loves McDonald®'s Restaurant	100	❑	❑
	Fun at McDonald's (BARBIE® doll)	45	❑	❑
	Fun at McDonald's (Ken® doll)	45	❑	❑
	Fun at McDonald's (Skipper doll)	45	❑	❑
203	Pepsi™ Spirit BARBIE® doll	110	❑	❑
	Pepsi™ Spirit Skipper doll	110	❑	❑
204	Ice Capades 50th Anniversary BARBIE® Pendant	22	❑	❑
205	United Colors of Benetton BARBIE® doll	35	❑	❑
206	All-American BARBIE® doll	35	❑	❑
	All-American Ken® doll	32	❑	❑
207	BARBIE® Flintstones Funwear Gift Set	10	❑	❑
208	Happy Meal Stacie doll	22	❑	❑
	Happy Meal Todd doll	22	❑	❑
209	BARBIE® Mustang™	50	❑	❑
	Me and My Mustang™! BARBIE® doll	50	❑	❑
211	BARBIE® Fun Fixin'™ Cake Set (Retail)	7	❑	❑
213	BARBIE® Fun Fixin'™ Barbecue Set (Retail)	7	❑	❑
214	BARBIE® Fun Fixin'™ Dinner Set (Retail)	7	❑	❑
215	BARBIE® So Much To Do!™, Cleanin' House (Retail)	6	❑	❑
216	BARBIE® Lee™ Jeans Fashions (Retail)	3	❑	❑
217	Pizza Party! Skipper's Pizza Shop	22	❑	❑
218	Got Milk™? BARBIE® doll	25	❑	❑
219	Coca-Cola Catalog - Holiday 1996	5	❑	❑
	Soda Fountain Sweetheart™ BARBIE® doll	95	❑	❑
220	Cool Shavin'™ Ken doll (Retail)	15	❑	❑
221	Russell Stover Easter Basket with doll	12	❑	❑
	CHAPTER 11 — MATTEL, INC. AND THE WALT DISNEY COMPANY			
222	Euro-Disney, Disney Weekend BARBIE® doll	100	❑	❑
223	Child World/Children's Palace Disney BARBIE® doll	75	❑	❑
224	Disney Fun™ BARBIE® doll, 1st in series	65	❑	❑
225	Disney Fun™ BARBIE® doll, 2nd in series	45	❑	❑
226	Disney Fun™ BARBIE® doll, 3rd in series	50	❑	❑
227	Walt Disney World BARBIE® doll	40	❑	❑
228	Mickey's Toontown™ Stacie doll	35	❑	❑
229	American Indian Barbie doll	$25	❑	❑
	Powhatan Village Playset	14	❑	❑
230	Disney's 101 Dalmatians Basket O' Puppies	25	❑	❑
231	Barbie & Friends Gift Set - Dressin' up with Mickey, Minnie, & Donald!	85	❑	❑
	CHAPTER 12 — MATTEL, INC. AND THE TRADITIONS OF THE OLYMPICS			
233	BARBIE® fashion, #7244 Get-Ups 'N Go - Olympic Parade	$68	❑	❑
234	BARBIE® Olympic Ski Village	65	❑	❑
	Gold Medal™ BARBIE® Skier	120	❑	❑
	Gold Medal™ Ken Skier	115	❑	❑
235	Gold Medal BARBIE® doll	80	❑	❑
	Skipper fashion, #7274 Best Buy - Olympic Swimsuit	40	❑	❑
236	Olympic Gymnast Set for BARBIE® and P. J. dolls	50	❑	❑
	Gold Medal™ P. J. Gymnast	85	❑	❑
237	Olympic Gymnast BARBIE® auburn	38	❑	❑
	Blonde	14	❑	❑
	African American	14	❑	❑
238	McDonald's Happy Meal Display	50	❑	❑
239	Olympic Gymnast BARBIE® Figurine	12	❑	❑
240	Skating Star Barbie doll	100		

	CHAPTER 13 — HOORAY FOR THE RED, WHITE AND BLUE!			
241	Ken fashion, Best Buy #9132	$25	❑	❑
	Skipper fashion, Get Ups 'N Go #9165 Bicentennial Fashion Patriotic & Pretty	85	❑	❑
	BARBIE® fashion, Best Buy #9158 Bicentennial Dress	32	❑	❑
242	Army BARBIE® doll	55	❑	❑
	Mattel 1989 Collector Classic Catalogue	18	❑	❑
243	BARBIE® Salutes Our Armed Forces Advertisement	12	❑	❑
244	Navy BARBIE® doll	40	❑	❑
245	Air Force BARBIE® doll	40	❑	❑
246	Marine Corps BARBIE® & Ken® Deluxe Set	80	❑	❑
247	Army BARBIE® & Ken® Deluxe Set	75	❑	❑
248	Air Force BARBIE® & Ken® Deluxe set	70	❑	❑
249	UNICEF BARBIE® doll advertisement	10	❑	❑
	UNICEF BARBIE® doll	50 each	❑	❑
250	BARBIE® for President doll	88	❑	❑
251	Astronaut BARBIE® doll	100	❑	❑
252	Statue of Liberty BARBIE® doll	75	❑	❑
	CHAPTER 14 — INNOVATIONS			
253	Color Magic BARBIE® doll	$790	❑	❑
254	Twist 'N Turn BARBIE® doll	185	❑	❑
	BARBIE® fashion, Winter Wedding	245	❑	❑
255	Talking BARBIE® doll	255	❑	❑
	Talking Ken® doll	180	❑	❑
	Talking Stacy doll	245	❑	❑
	Talking P. J. doll	185	❑	❑
	Talking Ken® fashion, Big Business	95	❑	❑
	BARBIE® fashion, All that Jazz	185	❑	❑
	BARBIE® fashion, Snap-Dash	145	❑	❑
	BARBIE® fashion, Knit Hit	100	❑	❑
256	Western BARBIE® doll	35	❑	❑
257	Magic Moves™ BARBIE® doll	48	❑	❑
258	BARBIE® Porsche® 911 Cabriolet (w/working headlights)	65	❑	❑
259	Sparkle Eyes™ BARBIE® doll	45 each	❑	❑
	Sparkle Eyes™ Ken® doll	35	❑	❑
260	Teen Talk!™ BARBIE® doll	50	❑	❑
261	Angel Lights™ BARBIE® doll	160	❑	❑
262	Twinkle Lights™ BARBIE® doll	60	❑	❑
	"Happy Birthday" Greeting Card	5	❑	❑
263	2-in-1 Porch Swing & Grill	45	❑	❑
265	High Stepper™ Horse (Retail)	30	❑	❑
	Puppy Ruff™	18	❑	❑
	Mitzi Meow™	18	❑	❑
266	BARBIE® Talking Colorforms™	25	❑	❑
267	Dance N' Twirl™ BARBIE® doll	50	❑	❑
268	Enchanted Evening, 1960 Nightlight	150	❑	❑
269	BARBIE® and Ken® Senior Prom, 1963 Musical	115	❑	❑
270	BARBIE® Boutique	100	❑	❑
271	Super Talk!™ BARBIE® doll	35	❑	❑
272	Ocean Friends™ BARBIE® & Keiko Gift Set	30	❑	❑
273	Leader of the Pack Motorcycle	50	❑	❑
	CHAPTER 15 — BARBIE® DOLL'S DESIGNER LABEL WARDROBE			
274	#7931 - Red Velvet Evening Cape	$155	❑	❑
	#7932-Metallic and Red Velvet Gown	155	❑	❑
	#7934- Pink Azalea Colored Gown	155	❑	❑
275	Peaches 'N Cream BARBIE® doll	85	❑	❑
276	Oscar de la Renta Collector Series IV	75	❑	❑
277	Oscar de la Renta Collector Series V	75	❑	❑
278	Oscar de la Renta Collector Series VI	75	❑	❑
279	Oscar de la Renta Collector Series VII	75	❑	❑
280	Oscar de la Renta Collector Series VIII	75	❑	❑
281	Oscar de la Renta Collector Series IX	75	❑	❑
282	Oscar de la Renta Collector Series X	75	❑	❑
283	Oscar de la Renta Collector Series XI	75	❑	❑
284	Oscar de la Renta Collector Series XII	75	❑	❑
285	Gold Sequin, #5405-9992	1000	❑	❑
286	Starlight Splendor™	950	❑	❑
287	Platinum™	1050	❑	❑
288	Neptune Fantasy™	1175	❑	❑
289	Empress Bride™	1125	❑	❑
290	Benefit Ball™ BARBIE® doll	275	❑	❑
291	Hollywood Premiere™ Fashion	50	❑	❑
293	Fifth Avenue Style™ Fashion	50	❑	❑
294	Masquerade Ball™	895	❑	❑
295	Royal Splendor™	375	❑	❑
296	City Style™	185	❑	❑
297	Opening Night™	235	❑	❑
298	Flower Shower™ Fashion	50	❑	❑
300	Satin Dreams™ Fashion	50	❑	❑
301	Queen of Hearts	625	❑	❑
302	Savvy Shopper™	250	❑	❑
303	Evening Extravaganza	95	❑	❑
304	Goddess of the Sun™	275	❑	❑
305	Donna Karan New York™ BARBIE® doll — blonde	150	❑	❑
	brunette	160	❑	❑
306	Moon Goddess	220	❑	❑
307	Calvin Klein Jeans BARBIE® doll	100	❑	❑
308	City Shopper BARBIE® doll	100	❑	❑
309	Crystal Collection		❑	❑

	CHAPTER 16 — PAPER COLLECTIBLES			
310	1980 25¢ off Coupon	$12	❑	❑
311	"Who's Who: The Mattel Licensing Directory"	10	❑	❑
312	Success for All Seasons catalogue	20	❑	❑
313	Mattel Delivers The Answer Book	12	❑	❑
314	Mattel Toys 1984 Catalogue	20	❑	❑
315	Mattel Delivers The Answers 1985	12	❑	❑
316	Mardi Gras Advertisement	10	❑	❑
	Mardi Gras doll	200	❑	❑
317	Girls Toys 1990 catalogue	20	❑	❑
318	Prototype photos One-of-a-kind		❑	❑
319	Smithsonian Magazine - December 1989	25	❑	❑
	#5 BARBIE® doll	450	❑	❑
	Twist 'N Turn BARBIE® doll	195	❑	❑
	1977 SuperStar™ BARBIE® doll	75	❑	❑
320	BARBIE® For Girls Decorative Border	8	❑	❑
321	Hallmark Cards, Inc. advertisement	10	❑	❑
	#1 BARBIE® Debut 1959 ornament	100	❑	❑
322	Snow Princess BARBIE®	140	❑	❑
	Valentine Greeting Card	5	❑	❑
323	Girls Toys — Celebrating 50 Years	20	❑	❑
324	BARBIE® Paperweight	100	❑	❑
325	BARBIE® 1996 Calendar (Commuter set)	10	❑	❑
326	Repro Art Book, 1996 Toy Fair Edition	20	❑	❑
	1996 Mattel Catalog	20	❑	❑
327	Enesco 1996 Catalog	5	❑	❑
328	BARBIE® 1997 Calendar (All That Jazz)	8	❑	❑
	CHAPTER 17 — AROUND THE WORLD WITH INTERNATIONAL BARBIE® DOLLS			
329	BARBIE® Doll International Collection Booklet	15	❑	❑
330	Parisian BARBIE® doll	$160	❑	❑
	Royal BARBIE® doll	230	❑	❑
	Italian BARBIE® doll	285	❑	❑
331	Oriental BARBIE® doll	160	❑	❑
	Scottish BARBIE® doll	155	❑	❑
332	India BARBIE® doll	150	❑	❑
	Eskimo BARBIE® from the Arctic	150	❑	❑
333	Spanish BARBIE® doll	145	❑	❑
	Swedish BARBIE® doll	130	❑	❑
334	Irish BARBIE® doll	145	❑	❑
	Swiss BARBIE® doll	115	❑	❑
336	Japanese BARBIE® doll	150	❑	❑
337	Peruvian BARBIE® doll	110	❑	❑
	Greek BARBIE® doll	110	❑	❑
338	(West) German BARBIE® doll, 1987	135	❑	❑
	Icelandic BARBIE® doll	120	❑	❑
339	Canadian BARBIE® doll	95	❑	❑
	(South) Korean BARBIE® doll	90	❑	❑
340	Russian BARBIE® doll, 1989	80	❑	❑
	Mexican BARBIE® doll	75	❑	❑
341	Nigerian BARBIE® doll	75	❑	❑
	Brazilian BARBIE® doll	75	❑	❑
342	Malaysian BARBIE® doll	75	❑	❑
	Czechoslovakian BARBIE® doll	155	❑	❑
344	Jamaican BARBIE® doll	65	❑	❑
345	Australian BARBIE® doll	50	❑	❑
346	Dutch BARBIE® doll	50	❑	❑
	Kenyan	35	❑	❑
	Chinese BARBIE® doll	30	❑	❑
347	Polynesian BARBIE® doll	45	❑	❑
348	German BARBIE® doll, 1995	30	❑	❑
349	Norwegian BARBIE® doll	40	❑	❑
	Ghanaian BARBIE® doll	30	❑	❑
350	Puerto Rico BARBIE® doll (Retail)	20	❑	❑
351	Russian BARBIE® doll, 1997 (Retail)	20	❑	❑
353	Native American BARBIE® dolls — 1993, 1st Edition	75	❑	❑
	1994, 2nd Edition	45	❑	❑
	1995, 3rd Edition	35	❑	❑
	1997, Toys R Us (Retail)	22	❑	❑
355	The Danbury Mint - plates			
	BARBIE® Visits Russia	35	❑	❑
	BARBIE® Visits England	35	❑	❑
352	BARBIE® Dolls of The World Stickers	3	❑	❑
354	McDonald's Happy Meal "BARBIE® Dolls of The World"	12	❑	❑
356	Native American BARBIE® ornament	22	❑	❑
	CHAPTER 18 — HAPPY HOLIDAYS SERIES			
	If any of the ornaments are signed; add 30%			
358	1988, holly berry red with silver trim	$900	❑	❑
	Happy Holidays doll advertisement, 1988	18	❑	❑
	BARBIE® The Magazine For Girls, Winter 1989	20	❑	❑
359	1989, snow flake white	375	❑	❑
	Happy Holidays doll advertisement, 1989	12	❑	❑
	BARBIE® The Magazine For Girls, Winter 1990	15	❑	❑
360	1990, fiery magenta (white)	160	❑	❑
	1990, fiery magenta (black)	145	❑	❑
	BARBIE® The Magazine For Girls, Winter 1991	15	❑	❑
361	1991, spruce green velvet	285	❑	❑
	BARBIE® The Magazine For Girls, Winter 1992	15	❑	❑
362	Mattel Report To Shareholders- Third Quarter, 1991	5	❑	❑
363	1992, silver	165	❑	❑

	BARBIE® The Magazine For Girls, Holiday 1992	15	❑	❑
364	3 Display Greeting Cards (1995)	30	❑	❑
365	1993, poinsettia red with gold trim	150	❑	❑
	BARBIE® The Magazine For Girls, N/D 1993	15	❑	❑
	Keepsake Ornament 1993 Displays	25	❑	❑
	Keepsake Ornament #1, 1993	150	❑	❑
366	1994, gold	250	❑	❑
	BARBIE® The Magazine For Girls, N/D 1994	15	❑	❑
	Keepsake Ornament 1994 Displays	20	❑	❑
	Keepsake Ornament #2, 1994	100	❑	❑
	1995, green lamé	95	❑	❑
	Happy Meal Holiday BARBIE® Figurine, 1995	28	❑	❑
367	Keepsake Ornament #3, 1995	35	❑	❑
368	Happy Holiday Collector Print	25	❑	❑
369	Happy Holidays Glass Ornament	35	❑	❑
371	Hallmark 1996 Club Ornament - 1988, Happy Holidays	50	❑	❑
372	1996, burgundy velvet	80	❑	❑
	Keepsake Ornament #4, 1996	25	❑	❑
	Keepsake Ornament 1996 Displays	15	❑	❑
	Hallmark Holiday BARBIE® Coloring and Activity Book	10	❑	❑
373	Matrix Happy Holidays Decoupage Ornament 1996	18	❑	❑
CHAPTER 19 — MISCELLANEOUS THING-AM-A-JIGS				
374	Deluxe Reading Dream Kitchen		❑	❑
	Large Household Appliances	$23 each	❑	❑
	Bits and Pieces	2-10 each	❑	❑
	Table	12	❑	❑
	Chairs	6 each	❑	❑
375	BARBIE® Thermos® Bottle, No. 2025H	85	❑	❑
370	Six-Piece Pewter Dinner-set	35	❑	❑
377	45RPM "Live Action" Records	10 each	❑	❑
378	The World of BARBIE® Thermos® Lunch Box with Thermos Bottle	70	❑	❑
379	Mattel Sew Magic Machine BARBIE® Fashion Set	85	❑	❑
380	BARBIE® Portable Phonograph	30	❑	❑
381	Small Household Appliances	20 set	❑	❑
382	Takara Photo-art Paper Dolls	4 each	❑	❑
383	BARBIE® Finishing Touches - Pretty Closets™	28	❑	❑
384	Avon - Holiday 1989 Catalog	5	❑	❑
	Avon Line, "I'm Into BARBIE®"		❑	❑
	Brush & Comb	12	❑	❑
	Cologne	6	❑	❑
	Bubble Bath and Dusting Powder	8	❑	❑
	Pierced Earrings	5	❑	❑
	Necklace	9	❑	❑
	Bracelet	6	❑	❑
385	BARBIE® Pretty Treasures		❑	❑
	Vanity/Dresser Set	10	❑	❑
	Picnic Basket Set	12	❑	❑
	Romantic Dinner Set	15	❑	❑
	Wedding Set	18	❑	❑
	Baking Set	12	❑	❑
386	BARBIE® So Much To Do!™ Paks			
	Gardenin' Pretty	8	❑	❑
	Cleanin' House	6	❑	❑
	Makin'Breakfast	6	❑	❑
	Country Fair Fun	6	❑	❑
387	Nostalgic BARBIE® Charm Pin	100	❑	❑
388	Long-Distance Greetings (Hallmark/Sprint)	30	❑	❑
389	BARBIE® Single Use Camera & Film All In One	10	❑	❑
390	BARBIE® Nostalgia Glamour Watch	40	❑	❑
391	Basic Fun Inc. - Keychain Series			
	Q.V.C. Exclusive Set	15	❑	❑
	Picnic Set	5	❑	❑
	Poodle Parade	5	❑	❑
	BARBIE® & Ken Set	8	❑	❑
392	Russel Stover Egg Shaped BARBIE® Tin	4	❑	❑
393	Classic Ornaments (Retail)	155 set	❑	❑
394	Russel Stover Heart Shaped BARBIE® Tin	4	❑	❑
395	BARBIE® and Ken Star Trek™ Gift Set	25 to 75	❑	❑
	Star Trek™ BARBIE® and Ken collector timepiece	30	❑	❑
CHAPTER 20 — HOW-TO-GUIDE FOR COLLECTORS ON SCENE COMPOSITION AND TIPS				
379 & 400	BARBIE® Feeding Fun Stable™ Playset	$17	❑	❑
	Nibbles™ Horse	17	❑	❑
396	BARBIE® Pretty Treasures™ — Wedding Set	5	❑	❑
	BARBIE® Fashion Avenue™ — Bridal Gown	10	❑	❑
	Ken® Fashion Avenue™ — Tuxedo	10	❑	❑
	Bridesmaid — #68065-95 Bridal Fashions	5	❑	❑
	Trademark Illustrations			
401	Swirl Ponytail BARBIE® doll, redhead	515	❑	❑
402	BARBIE® Fashion Accessories	35	❑	❑
403	BARBIE® and The Sensations™ Fashions — #4978 Poodle Skirt	30	❑	❑
404	Fossil Watch, Solo In The Spotlight — Sterling Silver	485	❑	❑
405	Golden Paper Doll Book — BARBIE™ #1502-5	5	❑	❑
406	A Little Golden Book — BARBIE™ and the Scavenger Hunt	2	❑	❑